*The Life We Are Given*

OTHER BOOKS BY GEORGE LEONARD

*The Decline of the American Male*
(with William Attwood and J. Robert Moskin)

*Shoulder the Sky* (a novel)

*Education and Ecstasy*

*The Man & Woman Thing, and Other Provocations*

*The Transformation*

*The Ultimate Athlete*

*The Silent Pulse*

*Adventures in Monogamy*

*Walking on the Edge of the World*

*Mastery*

*The Way of Aikido*

OTHER BOOKS BY MICHAEL MURPHY

*Golf in the Kingdom*

*The Kingdom of Shivas Irons*

*Jacob Atabet*

*An End to Ordinary History*

*The Future of the Body*

*In the Zone* (with Rhea White)

*God and the Evolving Universe*
(with James Redfield and Sylvia Timbers)

*The Physical and Psychological Effects of Meditation*
(with Steven Donovan and Margaret Livingston)

# The Life
# We Are Given

*A Long-Term Program for*
*Realizing the Potential of Body,*
*Mind, Heart, and Soul*

GEORGE LEONARD
*and*
MICHAEL MURPHY

Jeremy P. Tarcher/Penguin
a member of
Penguin Group (USA) Inc.
New York

JEREMY P. TARCHER/PENGUIN
Published by the Penguin Group
Penguin Group (USA) Inc., 375 Hudson Street, New York, New York 10014, USA • Penguin Group
(Canada), 90 Eglinton Avenue East, Suite 700, Toronto, Ontario M4P 2Y3, Canada (a division of Pearson
Penguin Canada Inc.) • Penguin Books Ltd, 80 Strand, London WC2R 0RL, England • Penguin
Ireland, 25 St Stephen's Green, Dublin 2, Ireland (a division of Penguin Books Ltd) • Penguin Group
(Australia), 250 Camberwell Road, Camberwell, Victoria 3124, Australia (a division of Pearson Australia
Group Pty Ltd) • Penguin Books India Pvt Ltd, 11 Community Centre, Panchsheel Park, New
Delhi–110 017, India • Penguin Group (NZ), Cnr Airborne and Rosedale Roads, Albany, Auckland 1310,
New Zealand (a division of Pearson New Zealand Ltd) • Penguin Books (South Africa) (Pty) Ltd,
24 Sturdee Avenue, Rosebank, Johannesburg 2196, South Africa

Penguin Books Ltd, Registered Offices: 80 Strand, London WC2R 0RL, England

Excerpts of five-line poem by Yamaoka Tesshu translated by John Stevens, page 159
of *The Sword of No-Sword* by John Stevens © 1984.

Most Tarcher/Penguin books are available at special quantity discounts for bulk purchase
for sales promotions, premiums, fund-raising, and educational needs.
Special books or book excerpts also can be created to fit specific needs.
For details, write Penguin Group (USA) Inc. Special Markets,
375 Hudson Street, New York, NY 10014.

Library of Congress Cataloging-in-Publication Data

Leonard, George Burr, 1923–
The life we are given: a long-term program for realizing the potential of body, mind,
heart, and soul / George Leonard and Michael Murphy.
p.   cm.
Originally published: 1995, in series: An inner workbook.
Includes bibliographical references.
ISBN 0-87477-792-5
1. Human potential movement.   2. Leonard, George Burr, 1923–   3. Murphy, Michael,
1930 Sept. 3–   I. Murphy, Michael, 1930 Sept. 3–   II. Title.

BF637.H85L46  2005                    2005048633
158.1—dc22

Printed in the United States of America
1   3   5   7   9   10   8   6   4   2

*Book design by Lee Fukui*
*Illustrations by Sergio Giovine*

*We dedicate this book to our fellow teachers in the experimental*
*Integral Transformative Practice classes of 1992 and 1993:*

ANNIE STYRON LEONARD
AND ERIK VAN RISWOLD

*and to the participants in the class who, through their devotion,*
*creativity, and perseverance, gave life to these ideas and practices:*

Sanford Anderson
Jani Ashmore
Pamela Carrara
Dan Carte
Walter Cole
Scot Combs
Niki Cronin
Alan Epstein
Anna Ernstthal
Robert Ernstthal
Lacey Fosburgh
Irwin Friman
Charlotte Hatch
James Hatch
Joan Herz
Linda Jue
Elizabeth Kelly

Donald Kerson
Kathie Kertesz
Leslie Lauf
Ruth Kissane
David Lombardi
Beth McCarthy
Chris McCluney
Linda Menicucci
Richard Moran
Phillip Moffitt
Roy Nakashima
Bruce Nelson
John Nicholas
Linda Novy
Bruce Orcutt
Jim Patrick
Stephen Perelson

Tyrone Polastri
Hollis Polk
Karen Preuss
Katherine Randolph
Andrea Rossman
Hubert Schmidt
Robert Sperber
Dan Svagerko
Sylvia Timbers
Janice Uchida
Neal Vahle
Debra Viall
Karen Wilson
Patrice Winchester
Lari Wolf
Mira Zussman

# Contents

# Joining the
# Evolutionary Adventure

Like the human heart, the world points beyond itself to something greater and more beautiful than its present condition. That something attracts us all, in different ways, and leads many of us to seek transformation. Does it secretly inform the entire evolutionary adventure? Could it be that the human heart and the world's heart are one in their self-surpassing? We believe that they are. As we grow in love and strength, we become vehicles for the world's growth. We bring new sustenance to our families, new joy to our friends, new light to our places of work. We enhance the physical things around us, and the earth itself.

Never before has humankind enjoyed so much knowledge about our evolutionary universe and the ways in which we embody its stupendous adventure. It becomes more and more evident that our own well-being is indissolubly linked to the health of society and our environment. It is possible, now more than ever before, to see that our own growth is rooted in, and furthers, the whole world's advance.

We are fortified in this perception by the emerging story of our universe. It is, we feel, the greatest story of our time, our story of stories, this immense panorama of universal evolution from the in-

*We live only part of the life we are given.*

M.M.

credible birth of space and time to the emergence of human culture. To various degrees, all of us are influenced by it, and each of us can turn to it for inspiration. Through transformative practices of the kind presented in this book, we can share the most fundamental tendencies of the world's unfoldment—to expand, create, and give rise to more conscious forms of life. Like evolution itself, we can bring forth new possibilities for growth, new worlds for further exploration.

The story of evolution, as it has been elaborated by modern science, is a new story for the human race. Though a few poets and philosophers had guessed that humans developed from simpler forms of life, the fact of evolution was not widely recognized until Charles Darwin published *On the Origin of Species* in 1859. The deeper implications of this enormous revelation are still dawning on us. Many physicists and biologists, for example, believe that something more than chance and material causes is involved in the universe's awesome journey. The world's advance from atomic particles to consciousness, from inorganic matter to the human awareness of God, is an event that confronts every thinking person, leading many of us to wonder, "What is impelling it all? Where is the universe headed? What is the relation between evolution and higher powers? Can the human race advance any further? Can it move closer to God?"

Since the nineteenth century, a compelling answer to these questions has begun to emerge among certain scientists, philosophers, and laypeople. That answer, we believe, will grow in the world's imagination, and it has guided the work described in this book. In simple terms, it can be stated like this: while remaining transcendent to all created things, the divine spirit involved itself in the birth of the material universe. The process that followed, the uneven but inexorable emergence of ever higher organization from matter to life to humankind, is then—at the heart of it—the unfolding of hidden divinity. Evolution follows involution. What was implicit is gradually made explicit, as the spirit within all things progressively manifests itself. In the words of the Indian philosopher Sri Aurobindo, "Apparent nature is secret God."

This idea has been developed in different ways by the German philosophers Hegel and Friedrich Schelling; by Henry James Sr., the father of William and Henry James; by the French philosopher

Henri-Louis Bergson; by the Jesuit theologian Teilhard de Chardin; and by twentieth-century thinkers such as Jean Gebser, Alfred North Whitehead, Charles Hartshorne, and Sri Aurobindo. The vision put forth by these and other philosophers reflects intuitions reported by countless people since antiquity that they enjoy a secret contact or kinship with the founding principle of the universe. The recognition of a reality ordinarily hidden but immediately apprehended as our true identity, our immortal soul, our "original face," our secret at-oneness with God is implicit in much Buddhist, Hindu, Platonist, Christian, Jewish, and Islamic thought.

The idea that divinity is present in all things, manifesting itself through the immense adventure of evolution, helps account for the mystery of our great surplus capacities, our yearnings for God, our inextinguishable creativity, our sense of grace in human affairs. It helps explain our quest for self-transcendence and humanity's proliferation of transformative practices.

For it is the case that people in every culture, and in every age, have invented ways to realize their kinship or oneness with divinity. Neanderthals held burial ceremonies, indicating their sense of an afterlife, and Cro-Magnon peoples, more than fifteen thousand years ago, left us cave drawings of shamanic figures. These Homo sapiens had developed an awareness of themselves in relation to things beyond. In this awareness, this reach beyond the ordinary world, there occurred an immense evolutionary leap. The universe awakened to its secret soul, its guiding presence and destiny. That awakening has been nurtured ever since through innumerable practices of transformation that have arisen around the globe.

Such practices appeared on earth long ago, through shamans such as those depicted in Stone Age cave paintings. There is good reason to believe that these first specialists of human society had extraordinary powers to overcome pain, understand others, and provoke ecstasy in themselves and their fellows. Around fires at night, they led ceremonies with chanting and dance and sometimes with hallucinogens. Through mythic narrative, they reenacted the world's creation and led members of their group through symbolic death and rebirth. In their spirit-body some of them flew to the gods, descended to the underworld, and remembered their secret identity. These first masters of transformative practice sustained humanity's intuition that mind and flesh can be transformed in the fire of our secret divinity.

Many peoples have preserved the spirit of Stone Age shamanism and have extended our reach into the unseen. On the Indian subcontinent, for example, inspired philosophers have enlarged our spiritual vocabulary, broadened our metaphysical imagination, and invented yogas now practiced in every part of the earth. The Indian witness to our latent divinity is typified by the Katha Upanishad:

> Finer than the fine, greater than the great, the Self hides in the secret heart of the creature. . . .
> Seated, he journeys far off, lying down, he goes everywhere. Realizing the bodiless in bodies, the established in things unsettled, the great and omnipresent Self, the wise and steadfast soul grieves no longer.

For more than three thousand years, India has been a laboratory for spiritual exploration, constantly illuminating our capacities for extraordinary life. Through the Hindu and Buddhist traditions that began there, its teachings have spread around the world. Today, its philosophies and practices are enjoying a great renaissance.

Transformative practices also spread from China and Japan, extending our sense of the sacred into the things of everyday life. China's feng shui encourages a reverent sensitivity to dwelling and landscape; its medicine and martial arts incorporate yogic and shamanic lore about the body's potentially luminous anatomy; its decorative arts convey the subtlety and depth of mystic insight. Japan's aikido, its gardening and home-building crafts, its arts of tea ceremony and flower arrangement, bring the illumination of Zen into the simplest things, reminding us that the physical world is suffused with enlightenment.

This diffusion of soul-awakening from the East is complemented today by the rediscovery of Western esoteric traditions. People of many intellectual persuasions have embraced the teachings of cabalistic and Hasidic mysticism, with their emphasis upon the divine splendor, the *zohar* that shines forth when we live in accordance with God. Sufism has had a similar revival. In both Islam and Judaism there are ways to find holy joy in daily life—around the dinner table, in the wedding bed, at our places of work. In the words of the Talmud and various Sufi writings, a good work, a good marriage, a feast among family and friends, can provide a foretaste of the life to come.

And the words of Christian mystics are being published in record numbers. The early desert fathers, orthodox Greek and Russian saints, medieval mystics such as Hildegarde of Bingen and Meister Eckhart, the Spanish ascetics St. Teresa of Avila and St. John of the Cross, Protestant ecstatics such as Jakob Böhme and George Fox, and other God-intoxicated people of ancient, medieval, and modern Christendom influence us today through their newly translated writings, their vivid examples of holy life, and their imaginative ways of self-transcendence.

*To learn is to change. Our destiny is to learn and keep learning for as long as we live.*

G.L.

Every sacred tradition is having a generative influence in the global village, stimulating countless people to embrace once esoteric ways of growth. This worldwide event has helped produce a momentous new stage in the development of transformative practice. For today, more than ever before, long-term human change can be understood and guided with the help of science. There are many reasons for this, among them new advances in the understanding of human psychodynamics; demonstrations of our capacity for highly specific change in psychoneuroimmunology, sports medicine, biofeedback training, placebo studies, and hypnosis research; new discoveries about the mind's ability to reshape motivations, emotions, and the flesh; and sociologists' demonstrations that each social group nurtures just some of our attributes while neglecting or suppressing others. Never before has there been so much scientifically based knowledge about the transformative capacities of human nature. This knowledge, combined with the lore and inspiration of the sacred traditions, gives us an unprecedented opportunity to make a great evolutionary advance. It is possible now, we believe, for humanity to pursue its destiny with more clarity than ever before. To quote the poet Christopher Fry: "Affairs are now soul-size. The enterprise is exploration into God."

Every person on this planet can join the procession of transformative practice that began with our ancient ancestors. That is the guiding idea of this book. The ways of growth described here, which can be adopted by anyone, embrace our many parts. We call them *integral* to signify their inclusion of our entire human nature—body, mind, heart, and soul.

When wisely pursued, such practices bestow countless blessings. If we do not obsess about their results, they make us vehicles of grace and reveal unexpected treasures. In this, they often seem paradoxical. They require time, for example, but frequently make more time available to us: they can slow time down, and open us to the timeless moment from which we have arisen. They require sacrifice, but they restore us. While demanding the relinquishment of established patterns, they open us to new love, new awareness, new energy; what we lose is replaced by new joy, beauty, and strength. They require effort, but come to be effortless. Demanding commitment, they eventually proceed like second nature. They need a persistent will, but after a while flow unimpeded. Whereas they are typically hard to start, they eventually cannot be stopped.

For most of us, integral practices require hard work. But with patience, the initial discomfort they cause turns into an ever-recurring pleasure. Renewing mind and heart, rebuilding the body, restoring the soul, enriching our relationships with others, become sources of endless love and delight.

*VISION*

*and*

*PRACTICE*

# A Lifetime's Quest

For years, the two of us had wanted to try out our ideas about the realization of extraordinary human abilities, to see if people with busy lives could change themselves for the better through long-term practice. Separately and together, we had worked for most of our adult lives inspired by the belief that all of us possess a vast, untapped potential to learn, to love, to feel deeply, to create, and that there are few tragedies so pervasive, so difficult to justify, as the waste of that potential.

Novelist James Agee wrote, "I believe that every human being is potentially capable, within his 'limits,' of fully 'realizing' his potentialities; that this, his being cheated and choked of it, is infinitely the ghastliest, commonest, and most inclusive of all the crimes of which the human world can accuse itself. . . . I know only that murder is being done against nearly every individual on the planet."

We are haunted by Agee's words. They bring to mind the victims of war, famine, and disease, of ignorance, poverty, and injustice. They point to the dogmatism that inhibits thought, numbs the feelings, and twists the perceptions of entire cultures. But the crime of which Agee speaks is not a distant phenomenon, not something "out there." It touches the lives not only of those trapped by injustice or material deprivation but also of those considered fortunate: our parents and children, our friends and sisters and brothers, ourselves. It is hard to imagine words more heart-wrenching than those of a close friend or relative who at the approach of death is heard to say, "I realize now I've wasted my life." Against the backdrop of the billions of years it took to give us our life and the brief time we have to experience it here, the dimensions of such waste are beyond calculation.

And this isn't just a private matter. It's hard to say how much of the world's neuroses, drug abuse, illness, crime, and general unhappiness can be traced to our failure to develop our God-given abilities. But surely people who are deeply involved in lifelong learning, in practices that encourage community, good health, and a sense of oneness with the spirit of the universe, would be unlikely to sink into the despair, unrest, and cynicism that lead to so many individual and societal ills.

Early in 1992, sustained by our faith in the human potential, we convened an experimental class in what we called Integral Transformative Practice (ITP). The experiment lasted for two years and provided material and inspiration for this book. But it isn't just this one class that informs our words, but rather the gleanings of a long journey, a lifetime's quest.

**In Search of the Human Potential**

In World War II, George Leonard served as a combat pilot in the South Pacific. During the Korean War, he was an analytical intelligence officer and then an air force magazine editor. This work brought him to *Look* magazine as a senior editor, where he reported on religion, politics, social change, and the cold war. His experience in covering the civil rights movement, from Little Rock to Ole Miss and Selma, helped shape his feelings about human potential and social change. As a native Southerner, he knew how deeply segregation had penetrated every aspect of Southern life. To witness "unthinkable" changes in a matter of years or months showed him that when the historic moment arrives some sort of transformation is possible and perhaps inevitable.

More than any other subject, education became the focus of Leonard's reportage and writing. He visited scores of schools and hundreds of classrooms preparing award-winning essays and special features on the subject, seeking that magical moment when a child flings up a hand and says, "I know! I know!" This firsthand experience with education and miseducation led him, in 1964, to embark on a ten-month-long project to produce a major *Look* essay under the title "The Human Potential." It was during this investigation, in February 1965, that he met Michael Murphy, whose Esalen Institute had opened in 1962 under the banner "Human Potentialities."

Murphy and Leonard were introduced at a dinner given by one of Murphy's friends. They stayed up most of the night talking, discovering that their interests and aspirations made a serendipitous match. Leonard brought knowledge of social and political movements, behavioral psychology, and brain research, Murphy of humanistic and depth psychology, of Eastern religion and philosophy. They started a series of conversations and brainstorming sessions that continue to this day. During one session, still in early 1965, they found themselves discussing the civil rights and free speech movements. In the heady spirit of the mid-1960s, Leonard proposed that there should also be a human potential movement, thus naming a movement that, in ways neither he nor Murphy imagined at the time, has touched the lives of millions of people.

## Esalen Institute's Early Years

In 1950, Michael Murphy was a Stanford University student when he took a class with Frederic Spiegelberg, a charismatic professor of Comparative Religious Studies. Spiegelberg was recently returned from India where he had encountered the famous sage Ramana Maharishi and the philosopher Sri Aurobindo. His lectures had a profound and lasting influence on Murphy, inspiring him to give up his pre-med courses and dedicate himself to the study of philosophy and the practice of meditation. He read widely in religion and psychology, focusing on visions of evolutionary development. In 1956 and 1957, he spent a year and a half at the Aurobindo Ashram in Pondicherry, India, where he deepened his meditation practice and confirmed his committment to personal and social transformation.

Murphy's family owned land on California's Big Sur coast, with redwood canyons, hot mineral springs, high cliffs, and magnificent outlooks on the Pacific Ocean. With Richard Price, a former Stanford classmate, Murphy started an institute there, which he and Price named after the Esalen Indians who had lived on the coast. In its first years, Esalen hosted seminars on Eastern thought and religious practice, Christian mysticism, shamanism, psychedelic drugs,

*Whatever your age, your up-bringing, or your education, what you are made of is mostly unused potential.*

G.L.

humanistic psychology, ecology, and other subjects loosely grouped under the banner of human potentialities and the education of the whole person. Historian Arnold Toynbee, theologian Paul Tillich, psychologists Abraham Maslow, Carl Rogers, Rollo May, and B. F. Skinner, philosophers Alan Watts and Gerald Heard, comparative mythologist Joseph Campbell, gestalt therapist Fritz Perls, family counselor Virginia Satir, creativity researcher Frank Barron, and pioneers of somatic education such as Charlotte Selver and Ida Rolf, among others, led programs at the institute. As time passed, the emphasis in these programs shifted from lecture and discussion to meditative, emotional, and somatic work, from a primarily cognitive approach to what Aldous Huxley called the "nonverbal humanities."

In 1967, Murphy started an Esalen center in San Francisco to reach people in their places of work. Esalen also pioneered holistic approaches to medicine, created a sports center that explored new approaches to sport psychology and physical fitness, and initiated a program of cultural and scientific exchanges to foster better relations between the Soviet Union and America. With grants from the Ford Foundation, the institute worked with professor George Brown to develop curricula for elementary and secondary schools that joined cognitive, affective, and somatic training. Brown called this program "confluent education" to denote its joining of mind, heart, and body, and started a graduate school to promote such education at the University of California, Santa Barbara. From its first years, the institute fostered work for social as well as individual development.

Murphy's experience at Esalen introduced him to many ways of growth derived from Eastern and Western religious disciplines, psychotherapy, somatic education, and other fields. And it confirmed his faith in human tranformative capacities. But this experience taught him, too, that people cannot make healthy and lasting changes without attention to the whole person, without long-term practice, and without solid social support. Programs for growth, he found, can go wrong in many ways.

## THE TROUBLE WITH INSTANT ENLIGHTENMENT

In those early days, both of us were impressed with techniques that seemed to transform lives in a weekend. For example, a man might have been holding some dark secret all his life, perhaps a childhood episode of sexual abuse, afraid that if it got out he would be ruined.

During an encounter weekend, primed by exercises designed to elicit self-revelation and encouraged by the intimate revelations of others, he would tell all to the group—and the sky wouldn't fall in. Instead, he would be praised and embraced as he wept tears of relief. Or an aloof woman might take a psychedelic drug under skilled guidance and discover beauty in the most mundane objects while perceiving what is unique and holy in people previously considered quite ordinary.

Some of these transformative experiences were aimed specifically at social reform. In 1967, Leonard and Price Cobbs, a black psychiatrist, began a series of interracial marathon encounters designed to get at the roots of racism. The first of these sessions, called "very likely the toughest encounter session that had ever been convened at Esalen," by Walter Truett Anderson in *The Upstart Spring*, set the format and style for a series of black-white encounter groups that followed over the next two years. The thirty-seven participants met for an introductory session on Friday night. Then at noon on Saturday, they began twenty-four hours of nonstop encounter, with meals brought in and no sleep.

By the time those long, sleepless hours ended, very little had been left unexposed, not the fiercest rage or the most well-disguised resentment, not the most manipulative games or the most subtle prejudice. As each level of prejudice and rage was uncovered, however, it only led to another, deeper level. In the last hours before dawn, a chilly fog rolled in from the Pacific and all hope for a breakthrough seemed lost in despair and desolation.

But sometime after sunrise, there was a shift in the climate, a feeling that something unforeseen would happen. The moment finally came when a simple act of kindness by a black woman to a white woman broke the barriers between the races, and soon the whole room was full of weeping, embracing people. Tears and hugs were common in this setting, but these were made possible only through uncommon stamina and the participants' courage to confront prejudice and rage in themselves. In the searing spotlight of race, these people, many for the first time, had glimpsed the fragile and tragic beauty of existence and their deep connection with others.

It was often like that, not just in the interracial groups but in other short-term, cathartic programs of the time. Many people came out of such experiences with the feeling that they were beginning a new life, that they would never again be the same. And in a way they were right. They could always bring to mind that brief time of awakening, of living in a different world. But when they returned to their old environments, their old ways of life, the memory lost its urgency and the learning ceased. Within a few days or weeks or months, most of them fell back into their old, familiar paterns. The interracial marathons were particularly dramatic, but even here, unless participants continued their practice of interracial understanding, the power of the experience faded.

In a culture intoxicated with promises of the quick fix, instant enlightenment, and easy learning, it was hard to accept one of the most important lessons that came to us out of those powerful but short-term experiences: *Any significant long-term change requires long-term practice, whether that change has to do with learning to play the violin or learning to be a more open, loving person.* We all know people who say they have been permanently changed by experiences of a moment or a day or a weekend. But when you check it out you'll generally discover that those who ended up permanently changed had spent considerable time preparing for their life-changing experience or had continued diligently practicing the new behavior afterward.

**The Transformative Power of Long-term Practice**

Our attempts to establish transformative programs that lasted longer than a weekend go back a long way. Late in 1965, Murphy started laying plans for a nine-month resident program at Esalen. Leonard and others joined him in formulating a practice for the mind, body, heart, and soul, with a core faculty and many visiting teachers. The curriculum would include not just cognitive training but also what Aldous Huxley called the "nonverbal humanities"—such activities as meditation, creativity training, encounter, movement, sensory awareness, emotional expressiveness, and inner imagery. Residential fellows would complete a project during the nine months of the program, something that would make a contribution to society. The first program began in the fall of 1966, with seventeen fellows, selected from around two hundred applicants.

All of life, especially the part that deals with significant innovation, is full of surprises. Shortly after the program began, Virginia Satir, the noted psychologist chosen as its leader, left for no apparent reason. The program limped along for a while and finally pulled itself together, but could not be termed a success. The 1967 residential program was another thing entirely: a colorful, controversial, and strongly focused experiment in radical human change. Led by Will Schutz, a pioneer in open encounter, the program became a laboratory devoted to pressing the limits of self-revelation. The U.S. space program was then nearing its climax and the twenty-one residential fellows, who sometimes termed themselves "psychonauts," were shooting for the stars of openness and honesty. Rather than trying to establish a regular, long-term practice, this program concentrated on breaking through personal and interpersonal barriers. It had high and low moments, successes and tragedies, and was described in several national media features. In terms of establishing a long-term education for the whole person, however, it was not what we had had in mind.

Our study of the transformative process continued. Leonard's 1968 book, *Education and Ecstasy*, was a manifesto for the transformation of American schooling. In 1970, Leonard resigned from *Look* to write *The Transformation*, a book about the transformation of society and the individual. Other books followed—on the transformation of sports and the body, on the transformation of sexualilty, and in *The Silent Pulse*, on the nature of the transformative process itself.

In 1970, shortly after he left *Look*, Leonard took up the Japanese martial art of aikido. In the thirty-four years since then, there has rarely been a week during which he has not practiced this art. He received his first-degree black belt in 1976, his fifth-degree belt in 1997. Aikido of Tamalpais, the aikido school he and his partners, Wendy Palmer and Richard Heckler, started in 1976 in Mill Valley, California, has produced scores of black belts. From shaky beginnings, it has evolved into an *aikidojo* known and visited by aikidoists from many parts of the world.

Far more than a physical self-defense art, aikido has profound philosophical, spiritual, and interpersonal implications. It is through his practice in this art, more than anything else, that Leonard has learned about the ups and downs, the long stretches of diligent practice with no apparent improvement, the ecstatic moments that seem to come from nowhere—in short, the enduring joy and transformative power of long-term practice.

From aikido have come nonmartial arts exercises designed to teach new ways of being in the world. Over the years, Leonard has introduced his version of this work, Leonard Energy Training (LET), to some fifty thousand people. The relationship between what we call "mind" and "body" and the potential of both for positive change becomes clear in LET. In 1981 and 1982, as part of an ongoing LET class at Aikido of Tamalpais, Leonard carried on a bodily transformation project that produced some interesting results, including a number of significant bodily alterations. Over a six-month period, for example, a woman experienced the healing of a congenital heart defect. A man in his late thirties increased his height from 5 feet 10 inches to 5 feet 11¼ inches. This transformative work continued with two-month-long, sixteen-hour-day, six-day-week Leonard Energy Training certification programs in 1983, 1984, and 1987 at Esalen Institute.

## The Future of the Body

In 1972, Murphy published *Golf in the Kingdom*, a novel about his encounter with Shivas Irons, a mystical golf professional who made the game a transformative practice. The book prompted people to write Murphy describing their own illuminations in sport. Among the experiences they described were feelings of merging with the environment, uncanny sensations of physical suspension, perceptions marked by superordinary clarity, sensitivity to others that seemed telepathic, and moments of unaccountable joy. Murphy had known that people have metanormal experiences in many walks of life, but hadn't appreciated how diverse these are. A second novel, *Jacob Atabet*, about an artist with a gift for psychophysical transformation, caused more people to send reports of dramatic mind-body changes. As these multiplied, they convinced Murphy that people harbor a wider range of metanormal capacities than is generally thought, and that these are strikingly similar to the extraordinary powers, the "siddhis" and "charisms," produced by Hindu, Buddhist, Christian, and other religious practice.

Murphy's interest in metanormal experience was reinforced by his own practice, which now involved distance running. Guided by Mike Spino, an innovative running coach who brought mental techniques and great emotion to his training, he began to compete in Seniors' races, including marathons. In 1983, he was third in the 1,500 meter race for fifty-year-olds during the National Masters Championships in Houston, running the race in four minutes and thirty-five seconds. In the same year, he won the fifty-and-over bracket in eleven of his thirteen races, at distances ranging from 800 to 10,000 meters. His training at the time, which with Spino included meditation and visualization, gave rise to experiences such as those his correspondents described.

Inspired in part by such experiences and the continuing response to his books, Murphy began to assemble an archive dealing with extraordinary human experiences. He was assisted in this by his wife, Dulce Murphy, and Jim Hickman, both of whom subsequently directed Esalen's Soviet-American exchanges; by Steven Donovan, Esalen's then-president; by Margaret Livingston, who became the project's principle researcher; and by funding from Esalen. George Leonard participated in this work from its inception, joining discussions of the project's findings and critiquing the conclusions Murphy drew from the archive materials as he wrote *The Future of the Body*.

The Esalen archive contains scientific studies of meditation, hypnosis, biofeedback, mental imagery, spiritual healing, fitness training, somatic education, martial arts, and other potentially transformative activities, as well as descriptions of psychosomatic changes that occur in disorders such as multiple personality and hysterical stigmata. In building this collection, Murphy was influenced by Frederic Myers, who pioneered the study of metanormal capacities and was a principal founder of psychical research, by William James and his *The Varieties of Religious Experience*, and by Abraham Maslow, who studied peak-experience. These and other researchers have created a field of inquiry that can be regarded as a natural history of extraordinary functioning. Murphy and his colleagues followed their example, gathering material from many sources, including Russian scientists they met through Esalen's pioneering Soviet-American Exchanges who were studying "hidden human reserves." The body of information they produced, which grew to more than ten thousand journal articles, monographs, dissertations, and books, provides massive evidence that dramatic alterations of mind and body, whether healthy, pathological, or merely curious, occur in virtually all walks of life.

This collection dramatizes the fact that human beings have extraordinary capacities for change, which operate both creatively and destructively. It also provides evidence that certain activities, or "transformative modalities," such as imagery, catharsis, and self-observation, are involved in most significant alterations of human functioning. Murphy came to believe that these operate in effect as transformative practices, even when they aren't recognized as such. For example, both false pregnancy and the development of weight lifters' physiques

*At the heart of it, mastery is practice. Mastery is staying on the path.*

G.L.

are facilitated by sustained emotionally laden imagery. Women with false pregnancy and championship bodybuilders alike typically imagine their somatic changes with great passion and consistency. Such deeply felt imagery is evident as well in effective psychotherapy, somatic education, and other disciplines. It seems that a limited number of such modalities constitute all enduring ways of growth.

And Murphy was led to three further beliefs. First, every human attribute can give rise to extraordinary versions of itself. In *The Future of the Body*, Murphy chose twelve attributes with which to illustrate this principle: perception of external events, kinesthetic awareness, communication skills, vitality, movement abilities, capacities to influence the environment directly, pain and pleasure, cognition, volition, individuation, love, and bodily processes. All twelve have metanormal expressions among men and women, young and old, in different cultures. Examples of these are presented in later chapters.

Second, most significant human growth results from practices that address the whole person. In *The Future of the Body*, Murphy defines tranformative practice as a complex and coherent set of activities that produces positive changes in a person or group. It is most effective when pursued for its own sake, and when it is *integral*, that is, when it embraces body, mind, heart, and soul.

And third, each of us has more latent capacities than is generally known, many of which resemble the extraordinary powers produced by religious disciplines. Recognition of these helps broaden our understanding of the human potential. It gives us more options for growth. Many are described in *The Future of the Body*, and several of them are discussed in this book.

## A Transforming Crisis

In 1989, Leonard faced a health crisis. Its resolution gave proof that an integral transformative practice can change the human body for the better. It started early that year when a routine treadmill test indicated a mild blockage in his right coronary artery. His cardiologist told him that it was not life threatening and that, essentially, he should go on with his life and come back in a year. Anyway, the treadmill test might not be right. "We don't like to do an angiogram [a much more accurate but invasive test] until just before the operation."

Leonard didn't take the test results lightly. Both his father and his father's father had died at relatively early ages of heart attacks, and his own younger years as a combat pilot and hard-driving journalist had been marked by high stress and high-fat food in equal quantities. But "come back in a year" and "the operation" surely didn't exhaust all possibilities for dealing with the situation. Leonard contacted his friend Dean Ornish, a physician who was running a study on reversing coronary artery disease by lifestyle changes, without drugs or surgery.

Ornish's study involved twenty-two heart patients in a treatment group and nineteen in a control group, all of whom had shown arterial blockage on angiograms. Members of the control group had continued with their conventional coronary care. Members of the treatment group had committed themselves to an introductory weeklong retreat and two four-hour meetings every week for at least a year. At the meetings, also attended by their spouses, they took a forty-five-minute walk followed by fifteen minutes of cool-down exercises, then did yoga, meditation, and mental imagery for an hour. After a vegetarian, very-low-fat dinner, they participated in an hour-long group meeting facilitated by Ornish or staff psychologist Jim Billings during which they aired their feelings. They continued the exercise, yoga, and diet during the other five days of the week.

Ornish had taken on a tough one. The plaque that blocks blood flow to the heart isn't just a coating on the inside of the coronary arteries, like the gunk that lines old pipes. It comes from changes within the walls themselves. White blood cells congregate, fibrous tissue forms, cholesterol and other debris accumulates, and the walls thicken and bulge inward. No wonder the medical establishment had long believed that, while this complex process could be slowed or possibly stopped, it could never be reversed. Some of the people in the treatment group had been advised to have bypass operations. Now they were not even to take cholesterol-lowering drugs.

Leonard met with Ornish, who showed him slides of some of the patients' angiograms and PET (positron emission tomography) scans, showing significant reductions in arterial blockages. Ornish suggested that Leonard get a PET scan, which provides a noninvasive way of accurately measuring blood flow to all parts of the heart. When this test corroborated the results of the treadmill test, Ornish invited Leonard and his wife, Annie Styron Leonard, to join their treatment group, not as members of the study but rather as participant-observers.

Thirteen months after his first PET scan, Leonard went back to the same facility for another. Beyond all his expectation, it showed up as completely normal. By then, the first-year results for all members of the treatment group were in, and most of them were quite good. Ornish reported the results in detail at the annual scientific meetings of the American Heart Association and in the medical journal *Lancet* and other medical journals. Now there was no way the medical establishment could ignore the evidence. The National Institutes of Health made a large grant—enough to keep the program going until all the participants had completed four years.

Actually, the Ornish program was even better than the scientific studies, by their very nature, could show. For example, arteries that were completely blocked were ruled out of the study from the beginning. No one would have dreamed that these arteries would begin to open—which in some cases is exactly what happened. Openings of completely blocked arteries couldn't be reported in the study. On his walks with members of the treatment group, Leonard also heard compelling firsthand accounts of positive changes in many aspects of the participants' lives—gout cured, eyesight and hearing sharpened, digestion improved, breathing difficulties cleared up. Even more significant, perhaps, were dramatic shifts in the participants' psychological attitudes. Ornish often said he was more interested in opening hearts than opening arteries, and there was no question but that hearts were opened.

From the outside, one is tempted to suppose that the very-low-fat diet is the chief factor in reversing heart disease. But statistical studies suggest that it is the combination of all four main elements—exercise, stress reduction, diet, and support groups—that does the good work. Those in the program would agree. But if pushed to pick one of the four that is finally the most important, they might well name the support groups and the general sense of community. Leonard's experience with the Ornish group deepened an understanding of the power of the group process that began with those explosive groups at Esalen in the 1960s.

The Ornish program was not perfect; a few of the participants who didn't participate wholeheartedly didn't show reduction in arterial blockage. But there was a strong statistical correlation between adherence and success in reversing heart disease. In other words, those who followed the program the most diligently got the best results, and vice versa. Ornish's work was particularly heartening to us, not only because of its immediate personal and social value, but because it dramatically demonstrated the power of what Leonard and Murphy were calling Integral Transformative Practice (ITP).

It was *integral* in that it dealt with the body (diet, exercise, yoga), mind (reading and discussions of articles and book excerpts on relevant subjects), heart (group process, community activities), and soul (meditation, imaging, yoga).

It was *transformative* in that it aimed at positive change in body and being, in this case a transformation that was generally deemed impossible.

It was a *practice* in that it involved long-term, regular, disciplined activities which, above and beyond any specific external rewards, were of value in and of themselves. Members of the Ornish treatment group often said that even if their hearts were perfectly okay they would continue with the program because the quality of their lives improved. Leonard got word of his normal PET scan after only thirteen months on the program, but he didn't quit the group. He stayed on for two and a half years, until he began the Integral Transformative Practice class that informs this book and that owes much to Dean Ornish and the brave men and women who have gone against the prevailing wisdom and have prevailed.

## Guidelines for Long-term Transformation

By the middle of 1991, Leonard's book on long-term practice, *Mastery*, was in bookstores and Murphy's *The Future of the Body* was about to be published. Murphy had been writing it for seven years, after immersing himself in the Esalen archives for eight years before that. His research as well as our own experiences with transformative disciplines had confirmed our belief that all humans possess great capacities for growth, and that these are nurtured best by integral practice. The prospect of such a practice for people with demanding work and family commitments had great appeal for us, and we began laying plans for an experimental class in Integral Transformative Practice that would put our ideas to the test.

We didn't have all the answers as we prepared to begin the project in January 1992, but we were willing to learn from experience, to correct mistakes. And above all else, we were unwilling to get locked in doctrine and dogma. Still, from our years of experience we had drawn certain basic principles for the enterprise of human transformation, principles that would guide us in leading the class and that continue to guide us today. Among them are the following:

*Lasting transformation requires long-term practice.* We have already touched upon this essential principle and will return to it more than once in subsequent pages. Leonard's book, *Mastery*, a required text for members of the ITP class, shows how quick-fix thinking has vitiated modern life and argues that any profound learning requires long stretches of dedicated practice with no seeming progress. Only now are we beginning to realize that those people we consider masters are generally marked by their willingness not only to endure the plateaus of the learning curve but to love the process itself, to find satisfaction in diligent, long-term practice for its own sake as well as for the gains it brings.

*The most effective transformative practices involve the whole person—body, mind, heart, and soul.* The idea of the whole person goes back at least to the ancient Greeks. Most Greek thought, in fact, was informed by a sense of the wholeness of things, a sense sometimes quite lost in the increasingly specialized, fragmented modern West. Mind has been cut away from body, the mental from the material realm. In most of our current education, mind is enshrined, body often neglected, heart ignored, and soul assigned to other venues. Our concept of *integral* sees body, mind, heart, and soul as separate windows to an underlying wholeness. For us, the body can be a wise teacher, a royal road to the subconscious, a mirror of the emotions, and a holy companion of the soul. Recent research in psychoneuroimmunology identifes specific mechanisms through which thought and feeling directly affect what we call body and vice versa. To attempt high spiritual experience without the wise counsel of mind, body, and heart can create the kind of imbalance that leads to spiritual tyranny. For us, in short, the key is *balance*.

*Transformative practices in this age are best guided by several mentors rather than a single, all-powerful guru.* As the putative embodiment of some remote human possibility, the guru holds great appeal for many seekers. But it is almost impossible for a person who is considered superior to others, or even perfect, to get the rich and honest feedback needed for balanced practice, for the correction of wrong turns, and finally for sanity itself.

We have had ample opportunity since the mid-1960s to witness the swift rise and catastrophic fall of several originally appealing but finally destructive guru-led practices. Clearly, human life has at times been enlightened and enriched by great teachers who have been considered avatars by their followers. But this is a bad time for gurus and cults. We believed strongly in multiple mentors relating somewhat in the manner of a college faculty, with a feeling of collegiality. To this end, we enlisted two additional teachers, Annie Styron Leonard and Erik Van Riswold, both of them aikido black belts and experienced workshop leaders. Each of the four of us would lead classes, assist one another, and provide invaluable feedback.

*Though practitioners at times must surrender creatively to mentors, community, and transformative agencies beyond ordinary functioning, the final authority always remains with the individual.* A certain surrender, a certain relinquishment of dubious certainties, of old patterns of thought, feeling, and action, is necessary for any profound learning. To question every statement of a teacher or habitually sabotage group efforts in the name of personal independence can be a tedious, finally trivial exercise in ego. Still, we strongly believe that the final authority resides with the individual practitioner. For the teacher or the group to tell the practitioner what he or she is feeling constitutes tyranny. Practitioners' experiences are valid for them. Teachers and community are very important for transformation, but transformed thoughts, feelings, and actions arise at the deepest level of individual being and are the responsibility of the individual.

In transformative practice, there is also surrender to agencies beyond ordinary functioning, to God or the spirit of the universe. Sometimes, it seems, we must give up our knowing for a higher knowing. The grace that brings seemingly unearned gifts often surpasses our powers of understanding. But even in this ultimate surrender, in which we might experience ourselves and the universe as one, we invoke balance and individual responsibility.

### The Path that Never Ends

A notice for the Integral Transformative Practice class appeared in the January–June 1992 Esalen Catalog, distributed in the fall of 1991. Announcements also went out to the people on George Leonard's mailing lists. Applicants began coming in for the ITP group that would begin on January 4, 1992—far more than we could accommodate. For the people we accepted, and for us, the months to come would bring life changes, large and small, and in that sense, something new and different. But in a more fundamental sense, we viewed ITP merely as an extension of a path that reaches back to the beginning of time and stretches out to a measureless future. In the East, it is said that any true practice puts us on a journey during which, for every mile we travel toward the destination, the destination is two miles farther away. We were ready to embark on such a journey.

---

Beginning January 4, 1992
An Ongoing Workshop
Sponsored Jointly by Esalen Institute
and Aikido of Tamalpais

*George Leonard, Michael Murphy,*
*Annie Styron Leonard & Erik Riswold*

In his new book, *The Future of the Body* (to be published in May 1992 by Tarcher), Michael Murphy raises the possibility that by gathering data from many fields — including medical science, anthropology, sport, the arts, psychical research, and comparative religious studies — we can identify extraordinary versions of most, if not all, our basic attributes. Murphy's research has shown that the most reliable path toward the realization of these extraordinary attributes involves regular, disciplined practice. He defines a transformative practice as a coherent set of activities designed to produce positive changes in a person or group. For a practice to be integral as well, it must aim to cultivate the physical, vital, cognitive, volitional, affective, and transpersonal dimensions of human functioning in an integrated way.

Beginning Saturday, January 4, 1992, Esalen Institute and Aikido of Tamalpais will jointly sponsor a weekly two-hour workshop devoted to the development of integral transformative practice. The workshop will be held at the Aikido of Tamalpais studio in Mill Valley, California, and will relate Murphy's findings to the practice of Leonard Energy Training (LET) and other mind-body disciplines. LET is an integral transformative practice inspired by the martial art of aikido.

Through LET and other practices, participants in the workshop will have the chance to explore personal development in the twelve aspects of human functioning outlined in *The Future of the Body*: perception of external events, somatic awareness, communication abilities, vitality, movement abilities, capacities to manipulate the environment directly, feelings of pain and pleasure, cognition, volition, sense of self, love, and bodily structure. Participants will be offered the opportunity to engage in an extended bodily transformation experiment (see George Leonard, *The Silent Pulse*, Dutton, 1986, p. 159ff), and there will be discussion of the applications of integral transformative practice to society at large.

Recommended reading: Murphy, *The Future of the Body* (Tarcher, in press), Leonard, *The Silent Pulse* (Dutton), *The Transformation* (Tarcher), and *Mastery* (Dutton).

---

*The notice for the class as it appeared in the*
*January–June 1992 catalog of the Esalen Institute*

TWO

# The Adventure Begins

We designed our new practice, not for full-time practitioners, but for people with family and job obligations. Those who met for the first class in Integral Transformative Practice (ITP) on Saturday, January 4, 1992, included a journalist and an attorney, a pediatrician and a playwright, a product designer and a landscape architect, a financial manager and a veterinarian, and a psychotherapist and a photographer. They were successful people who ranged in age from twenty-eight to seventy-eight; the kind of people who were willing to take on something new and adventurous.

We had selected our thirty-six participants from sixty applicants. We had made it clear during interviews with each of them that the class would be based on an educational rather than a therapeutic model, and we chose people who were in better than average physical and psychological health. There's no question that healing is transformational—often powerfully so—and we were by no means ruling out the healing possibilities of the practice. But we wanted to be sure that our applicants would be willing to work toward the realization of extraordinary states *beyond* what is considered ordinary good health.

For eleven months, this group (Cycle 92) would meet every Saturday from 8:45 to 10:45 A.M. at the Aikido of Tamalpais studio in

Mill Valley, California, a 2,000-square-foot, second-story loft with exposed rafters and large windows through which the morning sunlight streamed. A second group (Cycle 93) would meet for ten months in 1993. Members of both groups would also attend occasional evening meetings at participants' or teachers' homes to discuss their readings and would take part in one overnight stay at a retreat center in the country during the 1992 cycle and two in 1993.

A chilly, crystal-clear day added to the undercurrent of excitement that marked our first meeting. After introductions and some necessary business, which included signing the legal release forms required of everyone who participates in a marital arts studio, George Leonard made a brief talk, starting out by joking that their mission was "to go where no man or woman has gone before." Actually, he went on to say, much of what they would do might seem quite ordinary. We knew that among the people gathered there for the first class were several teachers of human development, and we figured that most of them, as well as we four ITP teachers, could undoubtedly lead the class in exercises that would provide spectacular, gee-whiz experiences in short order. But we felt that some exercises give only the illusion of significant change and can even interfere with lasting, long-term transformation. We held a strong belief in the transformative power—and the sacredness—of life's quiet virtues, including intellectual curiosity and integrity, a sense of the spiritual, unconditional love, healthy exercise, and devotion to practice. We were in it for the long run.

"Yes, we're going to have a good time," Leonard said. "We're going to have fun. But more important is learning to enjoy regular practice, finding satisfaction in the unembellished beauty of the commonplace, and learning to love the plateau, the periods when you seem to be making no progress, just as much as you love the inevitable spurts of learning and change."

He went on to tell the group that the teachers were hoping:

1. to work toward creating an integral transformative practice, one that is appropriate for the current American lifestyle;

2. through this practice, to offer every participant the opportunity to enjoy increased centeredness, health, and growth in body, mind, heart, and soul; and

3. to experiment with transformations of the body and of all human faculties, from the ordinary to the extraordinary or metanormal.

Throughout our first meeting and during subsequent meetings as well, we stressed the fact that our fundamental purpose was to create a *practice*; that is, a nontrivial activity undertaken on a regular basis primarily for its own sake. Our practice would be *integral* in that it would involve and seek to integrate body, mind, heart, and soul. It would be *transformative* in that it would aim toward positive, long-term personal change. We would experiment with transformations of body/mind/heart/soul that would range from the easily explainable to the extraordinary. In this experiment, we would all make written affirmations of desired transformations and keep careful records of the results. As mentioned in the previous chapter, Leonard had used affirmations in his 1991–92 bodily transformation projects with good results. We explained to the ITP participants that, for the sake of the study, we would ask them to make affirmations in four categories:

**Affirming the Transformation of Body and Psyche**

1. *Normal.* This affirmation would specify some measurable physical change that could be realized through normal means. A person with a waistline of 33 inches, for example, might want to take two inches off his or her waist, in which case the affirmation would be, "My waist measures 31 inches." This affirmation could probably be realized through diligent attention to diet and exercise. There would be no mystery about the outcome. We asked participants to make their first affirmation in terms of bodily changes that could be easily measured, not because we were emphasizing the body over the other factors in integral practice but simply to make the results of this particular affirmation as objective as possible.

2. *Exceptional.* This affirmation would involve some change in body, mind, heart, or soul that might not defy conventional scientific explanation but would be an exception to what is generally considered normal. As it turned out, for example, one fifty-nine-year-old man in Cycle 92, an avid sports participant, made the following Af-

firmation Two: "I have sufficient mobility, strength, and range of motion in my left arm, shoulder, and back so that I can serve a tennis ball in the 100-mph range and pitch a baseball in the low 80s." At the time he made the affirmation, limited mobility and strength in his left shoulder plus occasional back pain had reduced the speed of his tennis serve to the 60-mph range and his baseball pitching to the 40-mph range. By the end of Cycle 92, on November 21, he was serving a tennis ball in the 90-mph range and throwing a baseball in the 70-mph range—not quite what he affirmed but still, it seemed to us, exceptional.

3. *Metanormal.* In *The Future of the Body*, Michael Murphy defines extraordinary or metanormal functioning as "human functioning that in some respect radically surpasses the functioning typical of most people living today." The metanormal, as we see it, would be difficult to explain in conventional scientific terms. To put the distinction in perspective in purely physical terms: If a thirty-five-year-old person, 5 feet 6 inches tall and in good physical shape, increased in height by half an inch or even three-quarters of an inch, such an increase might be explained in terms of improved posture and would fall in the normal range (Affirmation One). An increase of an inch might still submit to conventional explanation but would be exceptional (Affirmation Two). An increase in height of two inches or more would be metanormal (Affirmation Three). Here let us say that we were by no means urging people to increase their height. We're using this example simply because it clearly delineates the differences among Affirmations One, Two, and Three. Most metanormal functioning, as we see it, involves a significant change in state, a qualitative rather than quantitative change. And most of the metanormal affirmations in our experimental classes turned out to aim for positive change not in the body but in the mind, heart, and soul.

4. *Overall good health.* The last affirmation was the same for everyone: "My entire being is balanced, vital, and healthy." We considered Affirmation Four the most important of all in that it would provide a mitigating influence on the other three. We did not want a participant to achieve any affirmation through unbalanced, undesirable change. For example, we would not want anyone to grow in height by two inches at the expense of stability in the joints and ribs,

nor would we want anyone to achieve out-of-the-body travel at the expense of mental stability. Good health was our overriding concern. Affirmation Four also served as a measure of Integral Transformative Practice itself. Any viable practice, it seemed to us, should increase balance, vitality, and general health.

We were well aware that this study of integral transformation could by no means qualify as a rigorous scientific experiment. There was no control group. And there were far too many and too many *different* types of variables. Still, we believed it would be valuable to keep careful and complete records of our results to learn how the participants' adherence to various elements of the practice correlated with their success in realizing their affirmations. We predicted, for one thing, that there would be a strong correlation between participants' overall adherence and their success in achieving their affirmations; in other words, those who followed the practice most closely would get the best results. To guide us in analyzing the statistics, we enlisted the help of Stephen Sparler, who had compiled and analyzed statistics for Dean Ornish's experiment in reversing heart disease.

## Guided by the Integral

Beginning with the first class meeting, we stressed the importance not only of balance within each of the four aspects of our practice—body, mind, heart, and soul—but also among the four. We believe that these four aspects represent different manifestations of a single and fundamental *identity* that is unique for each individual, the uniqueness of which is revealed in your DNA, fingerprints, voiceprint, brain wave pattern, scent, handwriting, your very way of moving and being. Your identity, in fact, manifests itself in every aspect of your life. To change one of these aspects is, to some degree, to change all. To ignore or downgrade one is to create an unbalanced practice, an unbalanced life. To think of one as opposed to another—the "unruly, lustful" body as a threat to the "logical, judicious" mind, to give a familiar example—is to falsely blame human nature for what actually springs from cultural limitation. Today we are learning that body and mind mirror each other, sometimes with exquisite fidelity.

Guided by a deep respect for the integral, we did the best we could to address every aspect of being. A typical class might begin with a session of "staying current," during which anyone with a pressing emotional problem could express it openly to the group and receive support and understanding rather than advice or reassurance. This could be followed by the ITP Kata, a forty-minute-long series of physical, mental, and spiritual exercises that will be described briefly below, then treated fully in chapters 6, 7, and 8. There would likely be discussions of the current reading assignment from *The Future of the Body* or *Mastery*, and the class would almost always include an exercise from Leonard Energy Training (LET). Several of the most important of these are described in chapter 11.

Briefly, LET leads practitioners into a change of context that creates a transformational possibility. In "Taking the Hit as a Gift," for example (see page 144), a partner sneaks up behind you and grabs your wrist with a shout. This represents any unexpected blow in your life, from losing a valued heirloom to losing your job or worse. In dealing with your startled reaction, you learn to avoid fighting back reflexively, denying your feelings, or falling into the victim's role. Instead, you learn to experience and acknowledge your upset by paying attention to the bodily sensations it causes. After that, you can change the context of the situation, experiencing the hit as a gift of energy that can empower you to deal with this particular blow—with energy left over for further positive life changes.

Some classes involved working directly with our affirmations, most notably through a process called "Focused Surrender," which combines highly focused imagery with moments of surrender and alignment with God or the universe, as described in chapter 5. We also spent considerable time together in meditation and often broke up into small groups to discuss various aspects of the practice or simply to share feelings without becoming judgmental. As the weeks passed, the group became a community. After each session, most participants adjourned to a nearby cafe to continue the discussions begun in class. More and more of them joined in social groupings. And we became more familiar with the ITP Kata, a single form that touched many points of our practice.

## The ITP Kata

The Japanese word *kata* means simply "form." Our usage in this case is similar to that in the martial arts, where the practitioner performs a series of predetermined moves in a certain sequence. Each move in the ITP Kata is designed to flow naturally into the next, balancing and warming up the body, articulating every major joint, stretching muscles and tendons, relaxing the body, and quieting the mind. These movements lead to a session of induction and imaging followed by ten minutes or more of meditation.

George Leonard started working on the ITP Kata in August of 1991, five months before the first ITP classes began. He tried it out with various individuals and workshop groups, revising and improving it. He drew on exercises from hatha yoga, the martial arts, modern exercise physiology, Progressive Relaxation, visualization research, and witness meditation.

Many of the movements of the ITP Kata are familiar, but the sequencing is unique, reflecting our belief that one should warm up the body and gently articulate the joints before performing stretching exercises; that the relaxation phase of every stress-relaxation cycle is important; that one should be deeply relaxed before beginning imaging; that meditation is deeper and more satisfying after the body is warm, articulated, stretched, and relaxed than if done cold; and that meditation can serve, to borrow a metaphor from photography, to "print" one's images of positive change.

Knowing that most of us lead busy lives, Leonard at first tried to hold the Kata to thirty-five minutes, but eventually expanded it to forty minutes. This is the minimum time within which the practitioner can do the full Kata without hurrying, but is by no means a limit. One can expand any part of it.

## Long-term Commitments

The Saturday morning group sessions were important, but made up only a small part of the overall practice. All participants committed themselves to attend meetings regularly and punctually and also to deepen their practice on the days between meetings. They further agreed:

- to maintain their individual autonomy and authority while committing themselves to the group in vision and practice, thus creating a powerful field of group intentionality that could aid and abet positive, healthy transformations of individual body, mind, heart, and soul.

- to do the ITP Kata at least five times a week.

- to do at least three hours of aerobic exercise every week in increments of at least thirty minutes. In addition, they agreed to do whatever flexibility, strength, balance, coordination, concentration, and relaxation exercises would be necessary to realize their affirmations.

- to be conscious of everything they ate. This meant, first of all, no unconscious snacking. It meant reading food labels. It meant eating deliberately, with full awareness of the contents, texture, smell, and taste of everything eaten.

- to read all written material assigned by the teachers and, commensurate with their own best judgment, seek to integrate it into their practice.

- to stay current in their relationships with teachers and fellow participants and to take care of emotional needs in appropriate and healthy ways.

- to include their affirmations in their Kata and to seek in all appropriate and healthy ways to manifest those affirmations in body and being.


## Relinquishing the Quick Fix

Considering the busy lives that class members led, attendance was remarkably good. A few people dropped out. Some felt there was too much interpersonal work. Some felt there was not enough. Others left because of changes in residence or job. During the first couple of months, we replaced the dropouts, six in all, from our waiting list. The twenty-seven remaining participants, plus the six we added, finished Cycle 92.

The most insidious and powerful enemy of our practice and, it seemed to us, of all long-term endeavors, was modern industrial culture itself, with its relentless celebration of immediate gratification. Amid the din of quick-fix appeals, it is difficult to learn about the efficacy and enduring joys of regular, long-lasting practice. To keep our consumerist economy afloat, it seems, people have to buy goods and services that they often don't need and sometimes don't really want. Television commercials glorify immediate gratification, showing life as an endless series of climactic moments with no lead-in or follow-through. The disproportionate number of climactic moments on TV is matched by our nation's disproportionate use of illegal drugs that produce immediate highs or oblivion. But we are hooked on legal drugs as well, with their promise of "fast, temporary relief," and we are served by a medical system that features quickie doctor appointments culminating in prescriptions for drugs or surgery, with little or no advice on long-term lifestyle changes that can prevent or reverse many medical problems.

*The essence of boredom is to find yourself in the obsessive search for novelty.*
G.L.

The quick fix is evident in many places: in socially approved gambling, in fast-weight-loss diets, in thrill-a-minute movie and television dramas, in audiotapes that "teach you" while you sleep, in how-to books that offer management skills in a minute and total fitness in a half-hour a week, in weekend management seminars that promise you an "action item" you can use in your office on Monday with no practice at all, in bottom-line management itself, in the whole credit-card economy.

And in self-development programs as well—those that shoot for catharsis, self-knowledge, and transcendence, all in a weekend, or even in a day. But we shouldn't consider this unusual in the least; all of us who have participated wholeheartedly in our society have become addicted to some extent to the quick fix. Perhaps the most significant discontent we encountered in ITP came from those who had participated in a number of big-bang weekend seminars and who urged us to push more strenuously for high moments rather than long-term practice. While the course in its unfoldment did occasion its share of catharsis, self-knowledge, and transcendence, we resisted the temptation to forgo our long-term emphasis and push for a series of climactic moments. Gradually, most of us settled into our practice. There was a certain amount of grumbling about having to do the Kata at least five times a week. But then some people began reporting that it was getting harder *not* to do it than to do it.

## THE FRUITS OF LONG-TERM PRACTICE

Cycle 92 class members made their affirmations on February 15, 1992. After writing all four affirmations, they signed and dated their papers, then filled out a "Record of Body Transformation" form. They copied their affirmations onto this form, precisely as written. This was followed by a description of the current condition addressed by each affirmation. A space was left blank for a description of each condition as of November 21, 1992, to be filled in at that time. The Record of Body Transformation forms were copied, with one copy going to the participant and one kept on file by the teachers.

On Saturday, November 21, the target date for the 1992 affirmations, all thirty-three participants who completed Cycle 92 filled out their Record of Body Transformation forms, describing the condition addressed by their affirmations as it was on that day. Then, comparing their present condition with what it had been on February 15, they rated the amount of positive change on a scale of from 0 to 10. If, to use a simple physical example, a person affirmed he would reduce his waistline by two inches and ended up reducing it by only one inch, he would give himself a rating of 5. Some affirmations, however, did not lend themselves to such purely objective measures. We spent considerable time over three class sessions preparing participants to rate all affirmations with integrity, avoiding either positive or negative bias. Comparing the participants' ratings with our own measurements and other observations, we concluded that they were as reliable as any self-ratings could be, probably better than most of those that are commonly used in epidemiological studies. On the same day, participants also completed an ITP Adherence Questionnaire, their third that year, and an Evaluation Form. The Adherence Questionnaire was designed primarily to determine how faithfully participants had fulfilled their commitments to the class and to learn how their adherence to the program correlated with their success in realizing their affirmations.

The most striking finding involved the strong statistical correlationship ($p$ = .0002) between adherence to the program and progress made toward realizing affirmations. This correlation jumped out at us, suggesting strongly that the people who followed the practice faithfully were likely to be the ones who successfully transformed body and being. The statistical analysis helped us evaluate our work, but it was the personal success stories that brought us the greatest insight.

To take one case, a thirty-nine-year-old psychologist made the following Affirmation Three: "My will is in tune with the Divine Will of the universe. There are no obstructions. All things flow to me and through me: love, health, wealth, success, and creativity." As to her condition at the time she made the affirmation, she wrote, "I am frequently in conflict over finances, writing ability, and my relationships with [a former teacher]." At the end of the year, she wrote, "This has been my most startling result. My financial situation has tripled as a result of my not plotting how it would resolve. My most serious interpersonal conflict has completely resolved from its state.... There has been an almost total shift in my attitude. From former attempts to 'make' things happen to an acceptance of whatever is presented and an acceptance of whatever I am feeling. I truly feel more flowing and internally without the former obstacles that caused me sadness. I no longer feel stuck."

## THE STORY CONTINUES

During the two and a half months between Cycle 92 and Cycle 93, we pondered the first year's lessons. We had reasons to believe we were on the right track, encouraged by the fact that those who most faithfully followed the program generally got the best results. We were also heartened by the participants' generally positive evaluations. In rating the elements of the program as to importance in enhancing their practice and value in their lives, participants gave top billing to the ITP Kata, the Leonard Energy Training (LET) exercises, the affirmations, and the readings in *The Future of the Body*—all of which we considered basic to the project.

We decided to stick with the basics in 1993. Rather than trying to intensify the practice or to load the classes with exercises that yield immediate, sometimes spectacular results, we proceeded even more slowly and patiently than in 1992, making sure, for example, that everyone thoroughly understood the affirmation process before making their affirmations, even if that involved considerable repetition.

Once again, our deliberate pace occasioned a certain amount of grumbling. From the outset, we had espoused nonauthoritarian leadership and free expression, and our participants were, for the most part, mature professionals with no qualms about speaking out. (Thirteen participants from Cycle 92 continued through the Cycle 93 training.) Now a small but vocal minority began asking for an "Advanced ITP" or an "ITP II." We listened and talked the matter over but essentially hewed to the idea of long-term, patient practice.

## A STRONG FINISH

The ITP class was built on a vision of continuing human evolution, including the possibility of dramatic transformations through long-term practice. Yet we grounded our most ambitious aspirations in the particulars of the body. For our 1993 training, seeking a purely objective measure, we replaced the "Exceptional" category for Affirmation Two with the most particular of measures: percent of body fat. The new Affirmation Two was the same for everybody: "My percent of body fat is significantly less than it was on March 27, 1993, and my lean body mass is equal to or greater than it was on March 27, 1993."

We selected percent of body fat as a measure not only because we could get objective measurements but also because of the clear relationship between a low percentage of fat and overall good health. We were impressed by recent studies showing conclusively that maintaining or increasing muscle mass and reducing fat could increase vitality and delay or prevent many negative effects of aging, as well as reducing susceptability to numerous diseases. In a time of rapidly rising health costs, this matter has serious socioeconomic implications. We made it clear to the class that we were interested in health, not weight loss per se. We were aware of that peculiar set of mind that equates any desire for a healthy, well-toned body with "narcissism"—a vestige, perhaps, of an old puritanism, of our lingering denigration of the body. For us, there are many body types, all of them sacred. We consider the body a reflection of one's essence, co-equal with mind, heart, and soul. Its health and vitality is not a trivial matter.

To calculate before-and-after body fat percentages, an experienced physiologist, Terri Merritt, made skin-fold measurements for all participants on March 27, then again on November 13. The results were encouraging. Between March 27 and November 20, the percent body fat of the thirty class members dropped by an average of 12.60 percent. (As it turned out, the four teachers averaged exactly the same reduction: 12.60 percent.)

The results on the other three affirmations were also encouraging. Participants filled out two questionnaires during the 1993 Cycle. Results from the final questionnaire (November 20, 1993) were used for statistical analysis. Thirty participants finished the 1993 Cycle and completed the questionnaire. The average scores for progress made toward realizing affirmations, on a scale of 0 to 10, are presented here, as compared with scores from Cycle 92. (The Cycle 93 scores for Affirmation Two are not comparable. In 1992, as previously noted, Affirmation Two was "Exceptional" on a scale of 0 to 10. In 1993, it was percentage change in body fat. Also note that the "Average of affirmations" is an average of all the individual figures, not an average of the averages):

|  | Cycle 92 | Cycle 93 |
|---|---|---|
| Affirmation 1 | 5.67 | 6.30 |
| Affirmation 2 | 4.30 | -12.60% |
| Affirmation 3 | 4.53 | 6.67 |
| Affirmation 4 | 6.58 | 8.30 |
| Average of affirmations | 5.30 (av. of all 4) | 7.09 (av. of 1, 3, and 4) |

In Appendix B, you'll find a complete set of Cycle 93 statistics along with a detailed analysis. Here we'll note only four points of interest:

1. Success on realizing Affirmation Four ("My entire body is balanced, vital, and healthy") was remarkably high and correlated to a statistically signficant extent to participants' adherence to every important aspect of Integral Transformative Practice.

2. Success on Affirmation Two (having to do with reduction of percent of body fat) correlated to a statistically signficant degree only to the amount of aerobic exercise a week and class attendance. This doesn't mean that factors such as diet and strength training were not important, but it does highlight the importance of aerobic exercise.

3. We found that consciousness, awareness, and focused attention related strongly to success in achieving affirmations. For example, participants' *awareness* of what they ate showed up as even more significant in their success in achieving affirmations than did *what* they ate.

4. Success for achieving Affirmation Three ("metanormal") is even higher than that for Affirmation One ("normal") and shows no statistically significant correlation to any adherence factor. This might be explained by the fact that the class members' metanormal affirmations included many that were not objective and thus easier to rate incorrectly. But a close examination of the results as reflected in the participants' prior and post states and behavior leads us to believe that this was not a major factor. The metanormal process, as we came to know it, often involved intentionality and what we might call grace, and was not always amenable to reductive explanation.

Even in the case of the purely objective affirmations, intentionality alone sometimes might have played a part. For example, one thirty-seven-year-old man reduced his percent of body fat from 11.1 to 8.3 (a 25.3 percent reduction) while making no change in his exercise regimen and actually falling prey to a craving for oil, consuming large amounts of french-fried potatoes over the last two months of Cycle 93. We couldn't be sure that such dramatic bodily changes as his could be attributed solely to participation in the class and all that it entailed rather than to specific adherence factors. We suspected, however, that this was indeed the case. In the end, we were left with a healthy respect for long-term practice and for the power, and the mystery, of the affirmation process.

## Cataracts, a Loving Heart, and a Mass Murder

Again, it was not so much the statistics as the participants' stories of their transformations that convinced us of the program's value. From the beginning, we had told class members that if they had any affirmations they considered too personal to make public they should write them on a separate sheet of paper. A number of people told us of great successes with these private affirmations—which never appeared in the statistics. Other stories also escaped the statistical net. There was, for example, the story of Charlotte Hatch's eyes.

Charlotte Hatch's maternal grandfather had practically gone blind from cataracts. That was before the operation was available. Her mother was operated on for cataracts in her forties, as were each of her three older sisters. "Have you got your cataracts yet, Charlotte?" her mother began asking her when she turned forty. At first she could say no with a clear conscience, but at forty-two, when she found she did have them, she didn't want to admit it. "No, not yet," she would say. Then she would change the subject. Finally, she began telling the truth. "All of you girls got my genes," her mother lamented. "Not one of you with eyes like your father's."

In January 1992, at age forty-five, Charlotte entered the Integral Transformative Practice class. For one of her affirmations, she chose to reverse her heredity: "I intend to see that the following circumstances have occurred by November 21, 1992: The lenses of my eyes are clear. . . . My eyesight is improving daily."

As instructed by the teachers, Charlotte went to her HMO for an eye exam to get a baseline for the experiment. When she told the doctor what she was doing, he was unimpressed. The cataracts, he told her, were not yet very large, but were right in the middle of the lens, and thus were sure to obscure her vision. An operation loomed in her future.

Despite her doubts, Charlotte participated fully throughout Cycle 92. When November came, however, she couldn't bring herself to go back for another exam. So she simply left her Record of Body Transformations for that affirmation blank.

Charlotte signed on for Cycle 93 and left any mention of her eyes out of her new affirmations. But from force of habit more than anything else, she continued doing the cataract imaging and induction. In the fall of 1993, she found herself needing a pair of prescription sunglasses but having no up-to-date prescription. Reluctantly, bracing herself for bad news, she returned to her HMO. But the doctor completed the exam without saying a word about her cataracts.

"*Don't I have them?*" Charlotte asked.

"No. Your left eye is totally clear, and there's a tiny deposit at about 10:30 in your right eye. But it's not big enough to be called a cataract."

The affirmations made by members of the 1993 ITP class were not limited to the physical. They also included wished-for transformations of mind and heart. For example, a highly successful criminal lawyer affirmed, "My heart is open. I radiate love to all people." On March 27 he wrote, "[My heart is] currently about one-half open." On November 20 he reported, "This affirmation was chosen as a last-ditch effort to save my disintegrating marriage. I devoted a great deal of energy, attention, and effort to saving this relationship, including: economic, psychological [effort], meditation, and just devoting my time to [it]. The results are that we are still together with a greater understanding and love for each other. Comparing where I was on March 27 and now, the score is a ten. . . ."

The improvement in balance, vitality, and health covered by Affirmation Four showed up in the ITP participants' increased ability to deal with the stresses of life—nowhere more dramatically than in the case of Karen Wilson, who played an important role in dealing with a mass shooting that made headlines all over the world. At 3:00 P.M. on July 1, 1993, a fifty-five-year-old former client with two semi-automatic pistols strapped to his suspenders, another pistol in one hand, and a bag of ammunition in the other, walked into the offices of the law firm of Pettit and Martin on the thirty-fourth floor of 101 California Street in San Francisco. He moved from office to office, from floor to floor, shooting people as he went, killing eight and wounding six before killing himself. On the thirty-sixth floor, Karen and a group of her fellow workers barricaded themselves in the personnel department offices.

"We knew the killer was at large," Karen told us. "We wondered if he was coming to get us."

Karen, who served as Pettit and Martin's personnel manager, had been doing Integral Transformative Practice for five months when the massacre occurred. She characterized herself as a high-strung person, but said that her practice had given her "a center, something with which to stabilize myself." When the killer's location was uncertain, she had a chance to see how she and her fellow workers reacted.

"There were people around me who panicked. A couple of attorneys were close to hysteria. But I never panicked. Not to say I didn't react, but I just knew I had a center. I could see how calm I was. I started doing things like calling around to other offices, finding out where people were, what they knew, and getting information flowing. It was more form than substance, but it was calming to people because they thought I was doing something. A lot of them came up to me afterward and said they really appreciated the fact that I had kept my head and tried to do something useful.

"Having my practice also helped me get through the aftermath. It was traumatic and people were very upset. Those of us in management were called upon to do a lot more work, longer hours. Having the practice was invaluable. It gave me something to go back to, no matter what happened. It changed my life."

## THE ENDURING JOYS OF PRACTICE

Since earliest childhood, we have been told we must practice in order to achieve our goals. This has led us to assume that practice is merely a means, not an end in itself, and indeed that much of what we do in life is of value only for what we will get out of it sometime later. In our ITP classes, we have certain goals—our affirmations, for example—and practice makes it possible to achieve them. But that is only part of the equation. We don't just practice to achieve our goals, we have goals in order to enhance our practice, for we regard practice as having great value in itself.

As might be expected, there was some resistance to a regular practice on the part of almost every participant. Resistance to any significant change, whether it be for the worse or for the better, is a natural tendency of all living organisms, and this often ignored aspect of existence will be treated at length in the next chapter. Some participants never overcame that resistance. A few dropped out. As the weeks stretched into months, however, most of us experienced an ever-increasing richness in our practice. If at first we resisted doing the Kata, finally the moment came when a day without it seemed incomplete. For some participants it was the sense of community, the feeling of being joined with others in a meaningful enterprise, that seemed most rich. For some it was the creation of a calm core, a center of stability in the midst of the ups and downs, the vicissitudes that mark life in the electronic age. For most of us there was the tingling, fully alive feeling that comes from good health in the broadest sense: the health of body, mind, heart, and soul. And for all of us there was the vision that first brought us together: the awe-some knowledge that the universe is embarked on an enormous journey of evolution and that each of us has a chance to make a positive contribution—no matter how small, how incremental—to that journey. It is, after all, the accretion of minute changes that ultimately powers the most startling evolutionary leaps.

When Cycle 93 ended on November 27, 1993, we stepped back to assess the results and implications of the study we had conducted and to write this book. Integral Transformative Practice, as we see it, is a work in progress, which will continue to develop. Still, we feel that what we learned from the class, added to the learnings of our two lifetimes, provides the guidance necessary to specify a practice now, one that not only will enhance individual lives but also will be of significant social value.

We have received much encouragement in our work, none more welcome than the response of class participants when the teachers stepped back. Dismayed with the idea that the class might end, a core group formed to keep it going. As of this writing, the Mill Valley group is in its eleventh consecutive year of practice. In addition, guided by this book and a videotape of the ITP Kata, groups have sprung up not only in the United States but throughout much of the world. In the pages that follow, we offer you instructions for joining them and us in our quest. You can form your own group or do the practice alone; ITP is a portable discipline. Becoming consciously involved in your own evolution and that of your culture can begin with something as simple as taking your first step on a path of practice—as you'll see in the next chapter.

*A*

*TRANSFORMATIVE*

*PRACTICE*

*for*

*OUR TIME*

# THREE

# Stepping on the Path

To begin any strong practice is to turn the pages of your life to a new chapter. Eastern wisdom sees practice, first of all, as a path (*tao* in Chinese, *do* in Japanese). For every mile you travel on such a path (if your practice is a profound one), the destination is two miles farther away. And would you really want it any other way? Think about it. The more you know, the more there is to know. By your very knowing, you help create more knowing. The knowing gets richer, more fascinating for as long as you live. The more you create, the more you can create. The more you love, the more you can love. A profound practice never ends.

In the Buddhist tradition, a practice is viewed sometimes as a path, sometimes as a stream. The metaphor of the stream invites you to imagine a strong but gentle current that is already there to speed your journey. Just to enter such a stream makes you a different person. Even if you should go back to shore, you would feel its power. You might enter the stream then return to shore many times, but if you keep practicing you're finally there for good—in the stream, on the path. Just to consider getting started expands your vision and lifts your spirit. Taking the all-important first step with a sincere heart can be a sort of enlightenment. It presages an evolutionary adventure, and offers inner peace. It is momentous, and it is nothing special.

Many fine practices, many paths, exist. In the words of the thirteenth century sage Wu-Men, "The Great Way has no gate. There are a thousand paths to it." Many, many activities can be considered practices—meditation, yoga, bodybuilding, mountaineering, devotional religion, various forms of service to others. Americans once spoke reverently about the *practice* of medicine or law, and these professions are indeed practices if they are undertaken for their own sake as well as for extrinsic rewards, for the fascination and service they provide, as an expression of the practitioners' inner essences. But if that practice is only a collection of clients, a way of making money and gaining prestige, then it is not truly a practice.

Even something as commonplace as gardening can be a practice if done for the sheer love of it, as an expression of the gardener's soul. It is a practice to garden with care for every shoot, every bud. It is a practice to develop a communion with everything in your garden, so that your roses, for example, are treated not as mere objects to be manipulated and used but as honored guests at the banquet of your life, so that eventually they will come to have the special look of flowers that are looked at with love.

But if you garden merely to impress the neighbors or win prizes with your roses, then, in the deepest sense, such gardening is not a practice. Paradoxically, the person who gardens as a practice, for the love of it, is probably the one who will impress the neighbors and win prizes.

## The Social Value of ITP

Integral Transformative Practice, as we have pointed out, is designed for people with busy lives. Unlike most practices, it aims to involve and integrate body, mind, heart, and soul. It is based on a vision of evolutionary transcendence and offers the possibility of positive changes in many aspects of your being. We also feel that it has significant social value. For one thing, the practice of ITP has greatly improved the overall health of the great majority of those who have undertaken it. Good health, it seems to us, is intrinsically valuable. But in today's economic and social climate, there's more to it than that. Without a significant shift toward a healthier way of life among its citizens, every advanced industrial nation now faces a fast-growing and perhaps unbearable strain on its health care system, no matter what system it adopts. Drugs and medical technology have produced marvels of healing and life support, but have also produced an exponential rise in health care costs and have, in many cases, prolonged suffering in life's final stages. The only solution, as experts in the health care field have long acknowledged, lies in changing the way we live. *In terms of social responsibility, the pursuit of good health is a moral act.*

The health care situation, however, only highlights the destructiveness of our prevailing way of life with its emphasis on immediate gratification, short-term planning, and the quick fix. The biblical admonition that "Where there is no vision the people perish" might have an unfashionably apocalyptic ring to it, and the ancient Eastern belief voiced by aikido founder Morihei Ueshiba that "Without practice a nation goes to ruin" might sound extravagant. But in the absence of vision and practice, our values—even our ability to talk about values—wither away. In the kingdom of the quick fix, the individual is most valued for her ability to consume. "The one who dies with the most toys wins" becomes an unexamined cultural affirmation, and the noble individualism that once occupied a central place in the vision of the West devolves from "I am" to "I want," creating a climate of selfishness and self-indulgence.

We believe that any long-term practice that encourages community and individual autonomy while aiming at the realization of positive human potential can be a healthy antidote to a frenetic, scattered, quick-fix way of life. We believe that people who combine their practice with job and family rather than remaining in isolation can make a significant positive impact on their communities and on the world at large.

It is not our purpose to argue that this particular practice is the best or the only one. We have said that many fine teachings can come your way, and we feel the choice is up to you. If you keep your vision clear, you can discover rich possibilities in many practices. As the nineteenth-century sword master Yamaoka Tesshu wrote of his own practice:

> *Do not think that*
> *This is all there is.*
> *More and more*
> *Wonderful teachings exist*
> *The sword is unfathomable.*

Whatever practice calls to you, answer that call wholeheartedly and generously. In Goethe's words, "Whatever you can do, or dream you can, begin it. Boldness has genius, power, and magic in it." If you

choose Integral Transformative Practice, here is the heart of it—
eight personal commitments adapted from the commitments followed
in the 1992–93 ITP classes:

### BEGINNING YOUR PRACTICE

If the practice and vision described in this book do call to you, then
it is time for you to begin. *You don't have to wait until you have learned
to do every part of the practice before beginning it.* If a child waited to
speak in full, grammatically correct sentences before beginning to
talk, he or she would never talk. Learning the practice is part of the
practice—and the learning never ends.

### THE EIGHT ITP COMMITMENTS

1. I take full responsibility for my practice and for all transformations of my body and being that flow from it. While
   respecting my teachers and fellow practitioners, I fully
   understand that I am the final authority.

2. I seek to join in community with other ITP practitioners.
   While maintaining my individual autonomy and authority, I commit myself to my ITP community in vision and
   practice. I understand that just two people can make a
   community. I also know that I can create a community
   through electronic networks, or even practice alone, bol-
   stered by the greater ITP community. [See chapter 13.]

3. I do the ITP Kata at least five times a week. I understand
   that, time permitting, I can lengthen any part of the Kata,
   and that extended periods of meditation at the end of the
   Kata and at other times of the day are recommended. [See
   chapters 6, 7, and 8.]

4. I accomplish at least three hours of aerobic exercise every
   week in increments of no less than twenty minutes. Three
   sessions of strength training a week are also recommended, but there is no commitment on this. [See chapter 9.]

Try to find at least one person to join you. Form a larger group if possible, but bear in mind that ITP can be done alone. An instructional videotape led by George Leonard can help you learn the ITP Kata (See appendix A for ordering instructions and for other resources to enhance your practice.)

Integral Transformative Practice requires very little in the way of special equipment. We invite people of all ages and states of physical condition to join this practice, doing whatever parts of it are appropriate for each individual. One of our greatest hopes, in fact, is to further a vision of tranformative practice for everyone, regardless of physical or financial status.

5. I am conscious of everything I eat. [See chapter 10.]

6. I develop my intellectual powers by reading, writing, and discussion. I thoughtfully consider the visions and the readings set forth in chapter 12 and, commensurate with my own best judgment, seek to integrate cognitive understanding into my practice.

7. I open my heart to others in love and service. I stay current in expressing my feelings to those close to me and take care of my emotional needs in appropriate and healthy ways, seeking counsel when needed. [See chapter 13.]

8. For each six- to twelve-month period, I make at least one affirmation having to do with significant positive change in my own being. I also make the following affirmation: "My entire being is balanced, vital, and healthy." I include my affirmations during transformative imaging in my Kata and seek in appropriate and healthy ways to realize those affirmations. [See chapters 4 and 5.]

## TRAVEL TIPS

The way to begin a practice is simply to begin. Don't wait for a change in the climate or a sign in the sky. Don't put it off until you "have more time"; most of us are probably already sacrificing many hours to that life-devouring device in the TV room or other forms of passive "entertainment," time that could easily be reclaimed. To get started, just step on the path.

So you don't yet know exactly how to do the ITP Kata? Do the parts you can do. Do the best you can do. It doesn't have to be perfect. You'll get better. Same thing with aerobic exercise. If you've been living a sedentary life, begin slowly and consciously. Starting out too fast is the commonest reason people stop exercising. *Remember, this is not a quick fix. Be patient. You're in this practice for the long haul.* Our consumerist society has effectively demoted, if not suspended, patience. The literature of the East, however, is loaded with sword master-and-apprentice stories that mythologize patience as the virtue of virtues. All have the same general drift. A young man learns about a master of the sword who lives in a far province. After a long and difficult journey, he presents himself at the master's door and asks to become his student. The master closes the door in the young man's face. Every day thereafter, the young man comes to sit on the master's doorstep, simply waiting. A year passes, and the master grudgingly starts letting the young man do chores around the house—chop wood, carry water. Months go by, maybe years. One morning, without warning, the master attacks the young man from behind and whacks him on the shoulder with a bamboo sword. The master has begun to teach alertness. At length, the master gives his apprentice his own sword and continues teaching him the art of using it. All along, the apprentice has been learning the essence of every profound practice: patience.

But you don't have to find a sword master to teach you patience. A few weeks from now, if you've simply been patient and practiced diligently, you'll be surprised and delighted when you recognize how much you've improved.

Every element of your practice will gather force with the development of your attention and intentionality. How do you become more intellectually interested and focused? Practice. How do you become a more loving, caring, emotionally expressive person? Prac-

*A certain naivete is prerequisite to all learning. A certain optimism is prerequisite to all action.*

G.L.

tice. How do you develop a sense of community and social service? Practice.

It's not that these various activities stand out as separate, time-consuming chores. In ITP, at best, the various elements naturally blend and become part of your daily life, informing and adding meaning to all you do. *You might discover, as did some of our class members, that you have more extra time after beginning this practice than before.*

## THE EFFICACY OF LONG-TERM PRACTICE

Top-level performance in any profound skill fills us with awe. To hear a master violinist in concert, for example, leads us to assume that such talent must be inborn, a gift from God. The primacy of talent in achieving mastery, in fact, has been assumed for centuries. Recent research, however, has shown that long-term focused practice, rather than talent, holds the master key to top performance in almost every field. This recent research is surveyed in a long article in the August 1994 *American Psychologist* by psychologists K. Anders Ericsson and Neil Charness.

In a study of violinists at respected music academies, Dr. Ericsson found that the top-rated violinists had practiced an average of about 10,000 hours by age twenty, the second-level violinists had practiced some 7,500 hours, and the lowest level violinists had practiced about 5,000 hours.

Ericsson and Charness show that even skills thought to be purely innate can be learned through practice. Perhaps the best example of a seemingly God-given ability is perfect pitch: the ability to correctly name each of the musical tones with no reference from a tuning fork or other instrument. Only one out of every ten thousand people possess this marvelous skill. Experiments show, however, that, with practice, almost every normal child between three and six can develop perfect pitch. The children, in fact, *prefer* to learn perfect pitch rather than relative pitch, which is the ability to recognize the relationship between pitches.

Focused long-term practice can accomplish miracles in many fields. Take short-term memory. Almost every psychology textbook repeats the "fact" that short-term memory is limited to around seven bits of information—the length of a local phone number. Dr. Erics-

*Mastery isn't reserved for the supertalented. It's available to anyone who is willing to get on the path and stay on it—regardless of age, sex, or previous experience.*

G.L.

son and his associates, however, have used long-term practice with college students to shatter this putative memory barrier in spectacular fashion. After fifty hours of practice, four of the students could correctly repeat up to 20 digits after a single hearing. Another student, a business major not particularly talented in mathematics, practiced for four hundred hours and was then able to remember 102 random digits after only one hearing.

Practice can clearly improve physical performance, but the extent of this improvement is illuminating. The 1904 Olympic Gold Medalist in the marathon, for example, couldn't qualify for this year's Boston Marathon, an event for which tens of thousands of amateur runners are now qualified. We could try to explain this disparity in terms of better nutrition, coaching, and equipment, but these factors pale against the fact that even topflight runners at the turn of the century trained for only a few months preceding the event. Runners today train all year long, every year.

Long-term physical practice, Ericsson and Charness point out, changes not only the body's performance abilities but also its shape and its very physiology, not only growing hundreds of miles of new capillaries but even changing the proportion of different types of muscle cells. Practicing activities that require quick, explosive muscle power creates more fast-twitch muscle cells. Practicing endurance activities creates more slow-twitch muscle cells.

Obviously, we aren't focusing integral practice on attaining perfect pitch, remembering random digits, or running marathons, but the effect of practice on these activities applies to almost all human learning and change. We believe that every human individual is unique, one of a kind, and that each of us is born with a genius that will manifest itself in wonderfully unique ways. There are geniuses of love and of service to others, geniuses of spiritual radiance and understanding, geniuses of extraordinary and as yet undefined abilities that will light the way to the next step in our evolution. But none of these capacities can be realized without practice.

### THE INEVITABLE HUMAN RESISTANCE TO CHANGE— AND HOW TO HANDLE IT

There's one more thing. Somewhere down the road, say three or four months from the time you begin, you might feel a strong and inexplicable urge to stop practicing. This generally occurs just when your practice is going very well, just when you're beginning to change in a noticeably positive way.

Don't be alarmed. Every one of us resists significant change, no matter whether its for the worse or for the better. Our body, brain, and behavior have a built-in tendency to stay the same within rather narrow limits and to snap back when changed—and it's a very good thing they do. Just think about it: If your body temperature moved up or down by 10 percent, you'd be in big trouble. Same thing with your blood-sugar level and with many other functions in your body. This condition of equilibrium, this resistance to change, is called homeostasis. It characterizes all self-regulating systems, from a bacterium to a frog to a human individual to a family to an organization to a whole culture. And it applies to psychological states and behavior as well as to physical functioning.

A simple example of homeostasis may be found in your home heating system. The thermostat on the wall senses the room temperature. When the temperature on a winter's day drops below the level you've set, the thermostat sends an electrical signal that turns the heater on. The heater completes the loop by sending heat to the room in which the thermostat is located. When the room temperature reaches the level you've set, the thermostat sends an electrical signal back to the heater, turning it off, thus maintaining homeostasis.

Keeping a room at the right temperature takes only one feedback loop. Keeping even the simplest single-celled organism alive takes thousands. And maintaining a human being in a state of homeostasis takes trillions of interweaving electrochemical signals pulsing in the brain, rushing along nerve fibers, coursing through the bloodstream.

One example: Each of us has about 150,000 tiny thermostats in the form of nerve endings close to the surface of the skin that are sensitive to the loss of heat from our bodies, and another 16,000 or so a little deeper in the skin, which can alert us to the entry of heat from hot objects. An even more sensitive thermostat resides in the hypothalamus at the base of the brain, close to branches of the main artery that brings blood from the heart to the head. This thermostat can pick up tiny changes of temperature in the blood. When you start getting cold, these thermostats signal the sweat glands, pores, and small blood vessels near the surface of the body to close down. Glandular activity and muscle tension increase to the point of shivering in order to produce more heat. And your senses send a clear message to keep moving, to put on more clothes, to cuddle closer to someone, to seek shelter, to build a fire.

Homeostasis in social groups brings additional feedback loops into play. Families stay stable by means of instruction, exhortation, punishment, privileges, gifts, favors, signs of approval and affection, and by means of extremely subtle body language and facial expressions. Social groups larger than the family add different kinds of feedback systems. A national culture, for example, is held together by the legislative process, law enforcement, education, the popular arts, sports and games, economic rewards that favor certain kinds of activity, and by a complex web of mores, prestige markers, celebrity role modeling, and style that relies largely on the media as a national nervous system. And though we might think that our culture is mad for the new, the predominant function of all this—as with the feedback loops in your body—is the survival of things as they are.

The problem is, homeostasis works to keep things as they are even if they aren't very good. Let's say, for instance, that for the last twenty years—ever since high school, in fact—you've been almost entirely sedentary. Now most of your friends are working out, and you figure that if you can't beat the fitness revolution, you'll join it. Buying the tights and running shoes is fun, and so are the first few steps as you start jogging on the high school track near your house. Then, about a third of the way around the first lap, something terrible happens. Maybe you're suddenly sick to your stomach. Maybe you're dizzy. Maybe there's a strange, panicky feeling in your chest. Maybe you're going to die.

No, you're not going to die. What's more, the particular sensations you're feeling probably aren't significant in themselves. What you're really getting is a homeostatic alarm signal—bells clanging, lights flashing. WARNING! WARNING! SIGNIFICANT CHANGES IN RESPIRATION, HEART RATE, METABOLISM. WHATEVER YOU'RE DOING, STOP DOING IT IMMEDIATELY.

Homeostasis, remember, doesn't distinguish between what you would call change for the better and change for the worse. It resists *all* change. After twenty years without exercise, your body regards a sedentary style of life as "normal," while the beginning of a change for the better is interpreted as a threat. So you walk slowly back to your car, figuring you'll look around for some other revolution to join.

No need here to count the ways that organizations and cultures resist change and backslide when change does occur. Just let it be said that the resistance is generally proportionate to the size and speed of the change, not to whether the change is a favorable or unfavorable one. If an organization or cultural reform meets tremendous resistance, it is because it's either a tremendously bad idea or a tremendously good idea. Trivial change, bureaucratic meddling, is much easier to accept, and that's one reason why you see so much of it. In the same way, the talkier forms of psychotherapy are acceptable, at least to some degree, perhaps because they sometimes change nothing very much except the patient's ability to talk about his or her problems. But none of this is meant to condemn homeostasis. We want our minds and bodies and organizations to hold together. We want our paycheck to arrive on schedule. In order to survive, we need stability.

Still, change does occur—in individuals, families, organizations, and whole cultures. Homeostats are reset, though the process might well cause a certain amount of anxiety, pain, and upset. The questions are: How do you deal with homeostasis? How do you make change for the better easier? How do you make it last?

These questions rise to great importance when you embark on a path of practice. Your whole life obviously will change, and thus you'll have to deal with homeostasis. Realizing significantly more of your potential in almost anything can change you in many ways. And however much you enjoy and profit from the change, you'll probably meet up with homeostasis sooner or later. You might experience homeostatic alarm signals in the form of physical or psychological symptoms. You might unknowingly sabotage your own best efforts. You might get resistance from family, friends, and coworkers. Ultimately, you'll have to decide if you really want to spend the time and effort it takes to get on and stay on the path. If you do, here are five guidelines adapted from George Leonard's book *Mastery* that might help.

*Your resistance to change is likely to reach its peak when significant change is imminent.*

G.L.

**Be aware of the way homeostasis works.** This might be the most important of all. Expect resistance and backlash. Realize that when the alarm bells start ringing, it doesn't necessarily mean you're sick or crazy or lazy or that you've made a bad decision in embarking on an evolutionary journey. In fact, you might take these signals as an indication that your life is definitely changing—just what you've wanted. Of course, it might be that you've started something that's not right for you. Only you can decide. But, in any case, don't panic and give up at the first sign of trouble.

You might also expect resistance from friends and family and coworkers. (Homeostasis applies to social systems as well as individuals.) Say you used to struggle out of bed at 7:30 and barely drag yourself to work at 9:00. Now that you're practicing ITP, you're up at 6:00 to do the Kata, then a three-mile run, and you're in the office, charged with energy, before 9:00. You might figure that your coworkers would be overjoyed, but don't be too sure. And when you get home, still full of energy, do you think your family will welcome the change? Maybe. Bear in mind that a whole system has to change when any part of it changes. So don't be surprised if some of the people you love start covertly or overtly trying to undermine your practice. It's not that they wish you harm. It's just homeostasis at work.

*Be willing to negotiate with your resistance to change.*  When and if you should run into resistance, don't back off and don't bull your way through. Negotiation is the ticket to successful long-term change. The long-distance runner, working for a faster time on a measured course, negotiates with homeostasis using pain not as an adversary but as the best possible guide to performance. The ITP practitioner keeps his or her eyes and ears open for signs of dissatisfaction or dislocation, but doesn't stop practicing. Better to play the edge of discontent, the inevitable consort of transformation.

The fine art of playing the edge involves a willingness to take one step back for every two forward, sometimes vice versa. It also demands a determination to keep pushing, but not without awareness. Simply turning off your awareness to the warnings deprives you of guidance and risks damaging the system. Simply pushing your way through, despite the warning signals, increases the possibility of eventually backsliding.

You can never be sure exactly where the resistance will pop up. A feeling of anxiety? Psychosomatic complaints? A tendency toward self-sabotage? Squabbles with family, friends, or fellow workers? None of the above? Stay alert. Be prepared for serious negotiations.

***Develop a support system.*** You can do it alone, but it helps a great deal to have other people with whom you can share the joys and perils of the change you're making. The best support system would involve people who have gone through or are going through a smiliar process, people who can tell their own stories of change and listen to yours, people who will brace you up when you start to backslide and encourage you when you don't. The path of practice, fortunately, generally fosters social groupings. In his seminal book, *Homo Ludens: A Study of the Play Element in Culture*, Johan Huizinga comments upon the tendency of sports and games to bring people together. The play community, he points out, is likely to continue after the game is over, inspired by "the feeling of being 'apart together' in an exceptional situation, of sharing something important, of mutually withdrawing from the rest of the world and rejecting the usual norms." The same can be said about many other pursuits—arts and crafts, hunting, fishing, yoga, Zen, the professions, and most certainly the practice of integral transformation.

And what if your quest is a lonely one? What if you can find no fellow voyagers on your path? At the least, you can let the people close to you know what you're doing and ask for their support.

*In the master's secret mirror, there is an image of the newest student in class, eager for knowledge, willing to play the fool.*

G.L.

***Follow a regular practice.*** People embarking on any kind of change can gain stability and comfort through practicing some worthwhile activity on a more or less regular basis, not so much for the sake of achieving an external goal as simply for its own sake. A traveler on the path of integral transformation is again fortunate, for practice in this sense (as we've said more than once) is the foundation of the path itself. Practice is a habit, and any regular practice provides a sort of underlying homeostasis, a stable base during the instability of change.

***Dedicate yourself to lifelong learning.*** We tend to forget that learning is much more than book learning. To learn is to change. Education is a process that changes the learner. It doesn't have to end at college graduation or at age forty or sixty or eighty, and the best learning of all involves learning how to learn—that is, to change. The lifelong learner is essentially one who has learned to deal with homeostasis, simply because he or she is doing it all the time. Lifelong learning is the special province of those who have a profound practice, those who travel the path that never ends.

### Miracles, Luck, and Practice

There's a popular teaching that flies the banner, "Expect Miracles." And why not? Life itself is a miracle: We are here on this wondrous planet. Children are born. We know joy and sorrow. The grass keeps growing. And there are many more miracles to come. If cosmology and biology teach us anything, it is that we live in a transformative universe. Nevertheless, if ITP were to fly a banner, it would be a different one: "Expect nothing. Be ready for anything." Beyond expectations, beyond miracles, beyond good fortune, there is practice.

And there is a paradox: For those who practice diligently, for those who practice because they love to practice, seeming miracles become commonplace. The story goes that Ben Hogan, one of the greatest golfers of all time, was questioned by a reporter after winning a major tournament.

"How is it," the reporter asked, "that under pressure you're able to hit so many miraculous shots?"

After reflecting on the question, Hogan answered: "I guess I'm just lucky."

"But Mr. Hogan," the reporter said, "you practice more than any golfer who ever lived."

"Well," Hogan said. "The more I practice, the luckier I get."

# FOUR

# The Powers of Affirmation

On the path of Integral Transformative Practice, our affirmations are clear, straightforward statements of positive change in body, being, and performance. They represent a firm contract with ourselves. They focus our best conscious efforts on transformation while seeking to enlist powers beyond our conscious understanding. They are written in the present tense to describe conditions as you intend them to be at some specified time in the future.

To take an example: Say you're a person who is often too busy or preoccupied to consider other people's feelings. You want to develop more empathy. Your affirmation could be "I enjoy a profound empathy for other people that sometimes appears to be telepathic." Present tense. It would not be, "I will develop my powers of empathy" or "I intend to be a more empathic person" or "To be more empathic."

By employing the present tense, the affirmation, "I enjoy a profound empathy for other people that sometimes appears to be telepathic," might seem to deny reality. Yes, right now, in the life you lead, you are by no means an empathic person. But your affirmation is not a denial of that reality. Rather, it is an instrument for creating a parallel, present-tense reality in your consciousness, a precondition for the affirmation work we use in ITP.

This consciousness of yours is nothing you can touch or photograph or measure with any known instrument, but it is nonetheless real. It exists in the universe. It is organized. It produces results. Your job is to create the condition of being an empathic person in the realm of your consciousness. This may be accomplished through language (repeating the affirmation silently or aloud), imaging (creating a strong image of yourself as an empathic person, one who listens wholeheartedly), and emotion (feeling what another feels). In this example, some part of the change can be accomplished simply through practicing being empathic with loved ones, acquaintances, or strangers—even if that practice seems at first pro forma. It's also important to open yourself to the magic of grace, that mysterious, seemingly unearned mediation that often comes when least expected (see chapter 5). But whether the mediation is practical and easily understandable or metanormal and mysterious, the concentrated intentionality triggered by the affirmation process is central.

Later in this chapter, we list guidelines for making your affirmations, and at the end of the next chapter, we describe exercises designed to trigger your unrealized transformative powers. But first, let us simply explain how the affirmations are to be written. We recommend that you not rush. Make notes. Think about your affirmations for a couple of weeks or more. Do they really fit your desires? Do you really want to commit yourself to these particular affirmations.

When you're ready, get a sheet of lined, letter-sized paper. Using a pen, write on the top: "I, [your first and last names], intend to see that the following circumstances have occurred by [a date six to twelve months from now]:" Skip a line and write your affirmations, numbering them. No need to use the "normal," "exceptional," and "metanormal" categories of our experimental classes. Just make the affirmations that are most important to you. Still, we recommend that you make no more than four affirmations for any period, with this last affirmation: "My entire being is balanced, vital, and healthy." We would not want any affirmation to be realized at the cost of balance, vitality, and health.

After writing the affirmations, read them carefully, then sign and date them. A sample is shown here. This is a composite, based on experiences of participants in our class.

When you have finished your affirmations, make a copy for a

> ### Sample Affirmation Sheet
>
> I, Jane Doe, intend to see that the following circumstances have occurred by September 1, 2006:
>
> 1. I enjoy a profound empathy for people that at times appears to be telepathic.
>
> 2. At work, I operate in the "flow" all day, working in a state of harmony with my employees and customers.
>
> 3. I experience illuminations in which I feel a oneness with all of existence.
>
> 4. My entire being is balanced, vital, and healthy.
>
> Signed, Jane Doe<br>October 1, 2005

friend to keep, if you wish, in case you should lose your copy. Then put the original in a convenient, safe place. Take it out to reread if you should become confused about the exact langauge, but don't obsess about it. No need to reread your affirmations every day. They're there in your life.

Though you'll be working with your affirmations throughout the affirmation period, this is all the writing you have to do: your affirmations are made. But it is important that on the same day you make them you also make a written record of your present condition in the areas covered by the affirmations. A record for those affirmations might read as follows on page 56.

Here again, you might want to make a copy for a friend. Keep the original of this record with your affirmation sheet. On the due date you've picked for your affirmations, make the appropriate measurements if you have affirmed changes in your body and performance, evaluate your progress in realizing those affirmations that don't lend themselves to objective measurements, and again make a written record. This record might read as follows on page 57.

After your first cycle of affirmations is finished, you might make

## SAMPLE RECORD OF STATES OF BEING ON THE DAY AFFIRMATIONS ARE WRITTEN

1. I have been told by family members and fellow workers that I sometimes don't take their feelings into consideration. I am aware that I put getting things done above the feelings of others. Part of this, I'm sure, is because my powers of empathy are poor. I've never given high priority to tuning in to others' feelings. But I have had experiences that could be telepathic. On rare occasions, I have anticipated exactly what another person was going to say.

2. At work, I am currently in the "flow" about an hour a day on the average. For me, "flow" is a state in which everything goes easily and my mind doesn't wander. In this state, I effortlessly stay focused on the task at hand. I don't feel hurried or harassed, and I experience a sense of synchrony with my employees and customers.

3. I have read about mystical experiences that bring a sense of oneness with everything. On two or three occasions, I have had a vague sense of this, but never to the degree expressed in the books I have read.

4. I feel my energy is too "forward." I tend to get ahead of myself. My vitality is good most of the time, but I sometimes have low energy at midday and early in the afternoon. I use coffee at lunch for an energy lift. I suffer moderate headaches at my forehead and temples once or twice a week. In general I consider myself quite healthy.

Signed, Jane Doe
OCTOBER 1, 2005

### SAMPLE RECORD OF STATES OF BEING ON THE DAY AFFIRMATIONS COME DUE

1. My empathy has greatly improved. This gives me and the people I'm with great pleasure. I attribute this mostly to practice. I have practiced tuning-in to others' feelings and have been delighted with my progress. As for telepathic powers—nothing new to report on this front.

2. As of this date, I am in the flow almost all day, with only short periods of time being the exception. Rather than compartmentalizing my day, which I believe was based on habit and fear, I surrendered that control. I replaced it with faith in the universe, new skills, and a centered confidence in myself.

3. On June 17, on a soft, sunny late afternoon, while sitting on a grassy hill near my house, I felt an unexplainable sense of well-being and remembered my affirmation to experience the mystical state. Focusing my attention on a tree across the valley below me, I said to myself, "I am one with all I perceive." In an instant, my state of well-being deepened into a joy I had never experienced before, and I was overwhelmed by a sense that I was one with everything I saw, every rock and tree and blade of grass. Everything they say about the mystical state is true. It brings a peace and joy that passes understanding.

4. Much improvement! I rarely have headaches now, and I've stopped using coffee. My energy feels more balanced. Being in the flow state so much, I'm not ahead of myself nearly as much as I used to be.

Signed, Jane Doe
SEPTEMBER 1, 2006

a new set. But don't hurry. Take a few days, or weeks, to decide what's good for you and what you really want.

But what if you have experienced little or no success on a certain affirmation? If you wish, you can simply include it in your new set of affirmations, wording it the same way or rewording it so as to better express your intention. Several members of our ITP class who stayed with the project for two years made identical or similar affirmations for the second year, with good results.

For example, Tyrone Polastri, a forty-six-year-old marketing consultant with a special interest in sports, affirmed a 50 percent increase in body strength for 1992. Due to a broken left elbow and serious personal problems, he made little progress that year. In 1993, he affirmed a 30 percent increase in body strength. He was tested in ten different exercises (bench press, biceps curl, leg press, etc.) as to the maximum weight he could move at the beginning of the class, then again at the end. During this period, he did strength training for sixty minutes three times a week; however, he missed eight weeks of training. As it turned out, his strength increased an overall 88 percent. Particularly significant is the fact that improvement showed up even in muscles not included in his training program. Since he was concentrating on upper-body strength, for example, he did no leg press exercises and did not change his bicycling activity from that of previous years. Yet his leg strength increased by 140 percent.

## QUESTIONS TO ASK YOURSELF BEFORE
## MAKING YOUR AFFIRMATIONS

***Does the affirmation really represent a change in me rather than in the external world?*** Affirmations as used in Integral Transformative Practice are not magical. They are statements of an intention to change your own functioning in a positive way, not to make the external world play tricks for you. We were dumbfounded when one 1992 participant asked if, in the metanormal category, he could affirm that he had won the California Lottery—twice. "That would be metanormal, wouldn't it?" Then there was the woman who wanted to affirm that her business would net her $150,000. This, too, was inappropriate. But by increasing the amount of time she was in the flow state or developing her intuition or becoming more balanced and centered, she might well contribute to the financial success of her business. In every case, we asked participants to affirm positive changes in their own functioning rather than in the external results of that functioning.

***Am I getting ahead of myself?*** A twenty-nine-year-old financial manager and neophyte golfer made this affirmation in 1992: "I play par golf consistently, and my drives are, on average, 200 yards long." This woman, whose drives then averaged 125 yards, was actually a long way from par. Closing the gap over a ten-month period was not beyond the realm of the possible. And her affirmation did involve her own functioning rather than outside forces. Still, we found it questionable. The process as well as the result is important. To drastically foreshorten or entirely bypass the journey of mastery is to forfeit much of the richness of life.

George Leonard started in aikido as a raw beginner at age forty-seven and was awarded his first-degree black belt five years and three months later. To have magically attained black belt rank in a few months time would have been to miss out on many joyous and poignant moments and to violate an essential rhythm of practice.

Still, this is a matter of degree. We would not want to discourage practitioners from speeding and enhancing improvements of their functioning. Learning involves short, spectacular spurts as well as long stretches on the plateau, and affirmations can shorten the plateaus without breaking the rhythm of practice. One person in the class, a competitive Masters' Class runner, had been trying for years to reduce his waistline in order to increase his speed and endurance. In 1992, he affirmed reducing his waist by one and a quarter inches. His chief device for realizing this affirmation was an especially vivid and persistent image of a "girdle of fire" around his waist whenever he was running. In just three months, with the girdle of fire image, his waist was smaller by two full inches—this without any changes in his diet or exercise regimen. This person was by no means bypassing his practice, having been a serious and disciplined runner for over twenty years. But despite all his prior training, such a sudden spurt of improvement in physical conditioning testifies to the generally unrecognized powers of affirmation and imaging.

When we see the body as a structure of heavy meat and bones, all we can do is cut it or drug it or otherwise manipulate it from the outside. But when we create a picture more consonant with modern

A Journal of Practice

*You can simply record the ITP activities you complete each day along with the state of your awareness during each activity. If you wish, you can also note your thoughts, reflections, emotions, and sensations. Such a record is most valuable during an affirmation period.*

physics and see the body as elegant, ethereal fields of waves joined in innumerable feedback circuits, then we realize that thoughts and feelings can set off sympathetic vibrations in it. The deeper vibrations connected with the power we have called "intentionality" can produce transformations in weeks, days, or perhaps even minutes.

And how about the woman golfer who wanted to shoot par? Her record of affirmations at the end of the year tells the story: "I do not play par golf (surprise!). My drives now range between 150 and 175 yards. Generally my game is more consistent, and I'm hitting it straight down the middle more often."

Our advice? Don't be greedy, but also don't be timid.

*Is the change a healthy one?* The word "health" shares ancestry with "heal," "whole," and "holy" and should serve as a watchword not only in making your affirmations but throughout your practice. Bear in mind that transformation can be negative and destructive as well as positive and constructive. Attention to good health is of the essence. We consider the affirmation, "My entire being is balanced, vital, and healthy," as a gold standard and safety net for all the others. At the same time, we feel it wise to examine each affirmation of its own in terms of good health. You would not want to develop massive upper-body muscles to the detriment of a balanced body. You would not want to develop the ability to take out-of-body journeys at the expense of mental stability. Even at best, transformation can involve destruction: the breakdown of old patterns in the creation of the new. Consider the overall health of body, mind, soul, and heart before making your affirmations. If at any time during the process you should feel your health is being threatened, you can always slow down or pull back.

In the 1993 Cycle, Hollis Polk, a thirty-five-year-old real estate broker, affirmed that she was 5 foot 4 inches tall. At that time, she was 5 foot 1¼ inches. To realize her affirmation, she would have to grow two and a quarter inches. We urged her to reconsider, but she was dead set on 5 foot 4. After two months, she reported she had grown three-quarters of an inch, but was suffering pains in her ribs and joints. At this point, she agreed to back off. By the end of the class, she had grown between an inch and an inch and a quarter, with no ill effects.

Good health is the bottom line, and in this matter it is also important—as we will point out more than once in this book—not to neglect what mainstream medicine has to offer. Take your flu shots, if indicated. Make prompt and intelligent use of the exquisite diagnostic instrumentalities and healing capabilities developed by our science. This practice aims to integrate worlds that some people foolishly attempt to separate.

*Ultimately, human intentionality is the most powerful evolutionary force on this planet.*

G.L.

**How will this change affect others in my life?** Say you affirm a significant increase in your personal autonomy, your ability to control your own destiny. Say the affirmation is fully realized. Previously you'd been very dependent on other people. Now you're making decisions for yourself and generally operating more effectively. Do you think family and fellow workers will be overjoyed? Well, maybe. Before making your affirmations, consider the likely effects on the people around you. Discuss your plans with those you work with and those you care for.

**Do I really want this change?** Am I prepared to live with it? There's an old saying: "Be careful what you ask for. You might get it." Are you really the kind of person who is willing to be taller or enjoy abundant energy or express your love openly and freely or get in touch with self-existent delight or manifest metanormal capabilities? Are you the kind of person who is willing to realize your latent powers? Are you willing to live with a fuller expression of beauty and creativity?

Sometimes we have to look deep inside to know how fearful we are of our own potentialities. This fear has roots in society's tireless efforts, covert and overt, to shape us within the boundaries of "normality," which in a mass society too often devolve toward the lowest common denominator. During his years of writing on the subject of education, George Leonard discovered that educators are sometimes even more threatened by exceptionally high abilities than by exceptionally low abilities in their students. One student in Virginia, for example, took home a programmed course in geometry and finished a semester's work in one long weekend. This left the teacher with the daunting question: What can I do with him the rest of this semester? And, if he should continue at this rate, how about the semester after that? If this mental transformation is threatening, how much more threatening are transformations of body, heart, and spirit?

To become consciously involved in an enterprise that may

presage further human evolution takes courage and a sense of adventure. As in all high adventure, there are risks and no certainty of success. But regular, disciplined practice builds a base camp of security and support. No matter how high you climb, your practice is always there, waiting for you. If you wish, you can photocopy this form (adapted from the Record of Affirmations form used by members of our experimental class) and use it to record your own success in realizing your affirmations. We strongly recommend that your final affirmation, in every case, should be "My entire being is balanced, vital, and healthy."

## INTEGRAL TRANSFORMATIVE PRACTICE
## RECORD OF AFFIRMATION

**Affirmation 1**     (Write affirmation here)

Description of the condition addressed by Affirmation 1 as of date affirmation is written. Note dates of measurements or tests if other than present date.

Description of the condition addressed by Affirmation 1 as of date affirmation is due. Note dates of measurements or tests if other than this date.

Your evaluation of change on a scale of 0 to 10. _____

(Write affirmation here)                    **Affirmation 2**

Description of the condition addressed by Affirmation 2 as of date affirmation is written. Note dates of measurements or tests if other than present date.

Description of the condition addressed by Affirmation 2 as of date affirmation is due. Note dates of measurements or tests if other than this date.

Your evaluation of change on a scale of 0 to 10. _____

(Write affirmation here)                    **Affirmation 3**

Description of the condition addressed by Affirmation 3 as of date affirmation is written. Note dates of measurements or tests if other than present date.

Description of the condition addressed by Affirmation 3 as of date affirmation is due. Note dates of measurements or tests if other than date affirmation is due.

**Affirmation 4**     (Write affirmation here)

Description of the condition addressed by Affirmation 4 as of date affirmation is written. Note dates of measurements or tests if other than present date.

Description of the condition addressed by Affirmation 4 as of date affirmation is due. Note dates of measurements or tests if other than date affirmation is due.

Your evaluation of change on a scale of 0 to 10. _____

❋

# FIVE

# Catching the Winds of Grace: More on Affirmations

"The winds of grace are always blowing," the Indian mystic Ramakrishna said. "But we have to raise our sails." Through grace we are granted such priceless gifts as self-transcending love, joy, and peace as well as those extraordinary capacities that lift us above the commonplace. With grace, all comes to us as if freely given rather than earned, spontaneously revealed rather than attained.

Every enduring religious tradition recognizes this feature of human experience. Many traditions see a personal God as the gift giver, but this is not always the case. Zen, for example, has no doctrine of an external god. Still, "Buddha-Nature" is analogous to the grace of a personal deity in that, as Zen patriarch Dogen tells us, it is "always and everywhere present," everlastingly available, endlessly responsive to our aspirations for new life.

In terms of the evolutionary vision that informs this book, the infinite possibilities of the Divine Spirit were *involved* in the universe from the very beginning. Evolution is the process through which these hidden possibilities are revealed.

Here is a paradox: Grace seems freely given, involving surrender more than struggle. At the same time, dedicated, long-term practice seems to predispose us to its gifts. The same paradox inhabits the matter of prayer, which is similar to affirmation in that it involves consciousness and intentionality. In his book, *Healing Words*, Larry Dossey surveys numerous studies of prayer in healing. Such studies suggest that *petition prayer*, in which one asks for specific outcomes, is not quite as efficacious in the healing process as is *prayerfulness*, in which one surrenders to the greater mystery and aligns oneself with God, as reflected in the simple prayer, "Thy will, not mine, be done."

Through our experiments with affirmations, we have learned that our students generally best realize their affirmations by practicing what we call Focused Surrender. This practice combines strongly imaging a desired outcome in the present tense, as if it already was happening or had happened, then totally surrendering to grace. Thus, to the extent that the affirmation process is analogous to prayer, Focused Surrender combines petition prayer with prayerfulness.

George Leonard coined the term Focused Surrender while working on *The Silent Pulse*. He noted that every episode of grace or "perfect rhythm" described in the book involved the unlikely marriage of trying and not trying, of zeroing in and letting go. It appeared that both focused intentionality and the surrender of ego were necessary for experiencing existence at such a fundamental level and creating what often appeared miraculous. It was at the moment of surrender, after intense concentration during these episodes, that grace became manifest. From 1973 through 1975, for example, a researcher named Duane Elgin conducted a remarkable series of exercises at Stanford Research Institute, attempting to influence a sensitive, heavily shielded magnetometer by his intentionality alone. The magnetometer measures changes in a magnetic field and records these changes on a moving sheet of paper.

The first few exercises generally followed the same course. Elgin would sit or stand a few feet from the magnetometer, where he could see the recording device, and would focus all the force of his will on the instrument, trying to influence it and thus make the needle move. He would continue this concentrated effort for twenty to thirty minutes, watching the needle tracing an almost straight line— but with no results. Finally, exhausted and exasperated, he would say to himself, "I give up." At that moment, the needle would start indicating a change in the magnetic field. These changes were by no means insignificant. In some of Elgin's exercises, the needle went entirely off the scale; to get such results by normal means would take a force estimated to be one thousand times stronger than that of the earth's magnetic field. Nor did physical distance lessen Elgin's effectiveness. In one instance, he was able to affect the magnetometer strongly from his home several miles away.

Later, Elgin learned to refine his technique. "I'd spend twenty to thirty minutes doing the best I could to establish a sense of rapport and connectedness with the instrument, and with great will and concentration I would coalesce that sense of connectedness into a field of palpable energy. I'd feel myself coming into the magnetic field and pulsing it to respond. Then, when there would be a moment of total surrender, the response would occur."

There's no question but that ego has great power, but it also has limitations. If we entertain the notion that the universe somehow already contains all information, all possibilities, and that each of us is a context of the universe from a particular point of view, then we might say that to create a sharply focused, vivid image of what we are seeking serves to "tune" our being to that precise possibility. But that's not enough. The striving, the ego still gets in the way. When we surrender, relinquishing the ego with its limitations, we open the way for grace: news from the universe, a direct connection with the divine.

However we explain it, Focused Surrender has served in our bodily transformation exercises since 1981 as our most effective process for realizing affirmations. Focused Surrender exercises can be used in a number of variations. We start with this basic exercise.

**Focused Surrender**

Find a carpeted or matted space where you won't be disturbed. Lie on your back with your feet about as far apart as your shoulders and your arms out a few inches from your sides, palms up. Close your eyes and breathe deeply, letting the incoming breath expand your abdomen as well as your chest. Feel the surface beneath you. Shift slightly, as if you are nestling deeper into this surface.

Now send a beam of awareness through your body, searching out any area of tension. Wherever you find tension, let it melt away, as if it is sinking into the surface beneath you then into the earth. After completing this process of relaxation, you will spend a few minutes on a special kind of breathing that will require your concentration—and your surrender.

Start by taking a deep breath through your nostrils, with your mouth gently closed, being sure to let your abdomen expand. After you have inhaled fully, part your lips slightly and *consciously* blow the air out. But do it noiseleessly, as if you are blowing a soap bubble away from you. Continue blowing the air out consciously until you have fully exhaled. Then gently close your lips and simply wait, fully relaxed, expecting nothing. This is your moment of surrender. The incoming breath will enter your nostrils of its own accord. You need do nothing at all. If you are in a complete state of surrender, *the precise moment of inhalation will come as a slight surprise*. After the inhalation has filled you, open your lips slightly and repeat the cycle, consciously exhaling, then closing your lips and waiting for the spontaneous inhalation.

In this process, you are joining the voluntary with the involuntary, the willed with the spontaneous, the conscious with the unconscious. In the timeless pause between the willed exhalation and the spontaneous inhalation, you can begin to experience that state of egoless not-doing that is the very essence of creation and grace. Continue with this mode of breathing for a few minutes, then let your breath return to normal.

Now place your left hand, palm down, on your abdomen. With eyes still closed, bring to mind one of your affirmations. Say it aloud several times. Then create a mental image of yourself and your life as it would be were the affirmation already realized. Make it real in your consciousness in your body. Flesh out that reality with as many feelings as you can. As soon as the realized affirmation becomes vividly present, let your left hand rise a few inches above your abdomen. Let it float there as if suspended, with no effort on your part. Focus intently on the image, holding it in your mind with all your will. Concentrate!

When you can no longer hold the image in place, simply *give up* and let your hand fall to your abdomen. Lie there in a state of grateful acceptance of whatever may be, with a feeling of total surrender, a sense of alignment with the divine spirit or with the universe itself.

Whenever you're ready, repeat the exercise. There's a good chance the image will become more vivid with repetition. It might well be that your left hand will begin to rise spontaneously, with no conscious effort on your part, accurately signaling the presence of a vivid image in your consciousness.

When you choose to end the exercise, remove your left hand from your abdomen and put it on the floor a few inches out from your left side, palm up. Lie there in a state of acceptance for a while, then deepen your breathing. Move your body around gently with increased awareness of the surface beneath you. Stretch your arms and legs and, if you feel like it, yawn. Then open your eyes and sit up.

*At best, concentration transcends effort.*

G.L.

### THE VOID OF SILENCE

For this variation, you'll need some instrument which, after being struck, will continue to resonate, the sound gradually fading away. A well-tempered bell or gong or chime will serve the purpose. If a piano is available, use a note in the lower register, with the sustain pedal down. An electric guitar can be set so that a note, once struck, will gradually fade away. An extra person, one not participating in the exercise, is required to sound the tone. This variation is appropriate for use with groups, even very large groups.

Start with the relaxation and breathing processes used in the basic Focused Surrender exercise. *Before* bringing an affirmation to mind, place your left hand on your abdomen. The extra person will sound the tone. When you hear it, let your left hand rise a few inches above your abdomen and float there as if sustained by the tone. Follow the sound of the tone as it descends into silence. Use all your powers of concentration as it becomes fainter and fainter. Let it take you down into the void of silence, the nothingness out of which all things arise. When at last, despite your best efforts, you can no longer hear the sound, surrender completely and let your left hand fall to your abdomen. Lie there doing nothing, thinking nothing, simply experiencing a state of total surrender. When the hands of everyone doing the exercise have fallen to their abdomens, the extra person will sound another tone. Repeat the process several times.

Now, leaving your left hand on your abdomen, bring one of your affirmations to mind. Repeat it silently several times. The extra person will then sound the tone. As soon as you hear it, let your left hand float up as before. At the same time, let your affirmation become vivid and real, as if fully realized. Hold this image with concentrated focus until you've descended into the creative void and can no longer hear the tone. (Concentrate on the image; the sound will serve to take you down into the void.) Then let your hand drop to your abdomen and *give up* your affirmation. Surrender completely. Lie there in a state of acceptance and alignment with the universe.

The extra person will sound the tone at least seven times. Then he or she will tell you to place your left hand on the floor and return to the world of ordinary consciousness, as in the basic exercise.

## CHANTING YOUR AFFIRMATION

This exercise can be done alone but is especially effective with a group. Find a place where you can speak aloud without disturbing anyone or feeling self-conscious. Start by sitting as you might sit in meditation, on a cushion on the floor or in a straight-backed chair, hands on your knees. Check your posture, which should have a feeling of groundedness, uprightness, and openness. Close your eyes and send awareness through your body, locating and relaxing the tense places. Choose one of your affirmations. With your eyes still closed, take three deep breaths, then say the affirmation in a clear and resonant voice and with strong intentionality. Take another breath and say it again. Continue for at least ten minutes—more if you wish.

A strong image of your affirmation as if already realized might come to your consciousness during this exercise, but this isn't necessary. Here, the power of words is what counts. At first, the words will have clear cognitive meaning. If meaning later becomes secondary to sound and if the sound of your voice is more like music than talk, be willing to let this happen. This exercise tends to gain transformative power with the length of time you can keep it going. You might find it rewarding to continue for quite a long while.

When you finish, whether alone or with a group, remain seated while taking three deep breaths. Then lie on the floor on your back with feet about shoulder-width apart and arms a few inches out from your sides, hands palm up. Simply lie there in a state of acceptance, thanksgiving, and alignment with the universe. Take your time reentering your workaday life.

## AS IF

Focused Surrender has proved to be a powerful modality for transformation, but there are others. Sometimes the best ways of realizing affirmations are the simplest. As you go about your daily life, for example you might simply act *as if* an affirmation has already been realized. Say you affirmed being open and loving at all times. Just ask yourself, "What does it feel like to be an open and loving person at all times? How does an open and loving person act?" You don't have to wait. You can start out immediately being and acting as if you are that person.

This doesn't imply denial. Yes, you know that you haven't achieved constant openness and lovingness yet. You slip. You fall. But that doesn't keep you from starting again. Which brings us back to the foundation of all enduring transformation: *practice*. How do you become an open and loving person? You practice.

On matters of physical change—becoming stronger or faster for example—you obviously can't start by literally acting as if you are, say, 30 percent stronger. But you can immediately start acting as if you're the *kind of person* who is 30 percent stronger or faster. You can ask yourself what it would be like if you were 30 percent stronger. How would you stand and walk? How would you approach people? How would your self-image change? How would your body feel? By repeatedly exploring these *as if* conditions mentally and emotionally, you can set the essential personal context for the change that's underway.

And keep in mind that while seeming miracles might happen through grace, the best context for both grace and miracles involves sincere, diligent practice.

## AFFIRMATION CHECKPOINTS

In the hurry and worry of daily life, it's easy to neglect what we most desire. A community of practice—even one other committed person—can help us stay on the path. Still, we forget. The electronic clamor that surrounds us, the unrelenting seductiveness of "entertainment," the hypnotic pull of sheer busyness all conspire against the awareness that furthers transformation.

To remind yourself of your affirmations (and of your overall practice as well), select two or three checkpoints in your house or workplace. Pick places you are sure to pass on a typical day—the door to your bathroom or kitchen, a staircase, the front or back entrance. To help catch your attention, you might mark your checkpoints. (The brightly colored paste-on circles available at office supply stores make good markers.) Eventually, you might become so accustomed to these markings that you no longer notice them. In that case, change the colors of the markings. Change the location of the checkpoints themselves.

Every time you pass one of these reminders, say an affirmation silently or aloud. Bring an image of the affirmation to mind. Act as if in some way it is already realized. Perhaps the words, the image, the *as if* state of being will stay with you for more than a short while as you carry on with your daily life. It might not be easy but it is possible to integrate your practice in some significant manner with your responsibilities to job and family. Affirmation checkpoints can jumpstart the process that produces such a fusion.

## A Possibility to be Realized

But it's not just our affirmations, or even our practice, that we forget. We become numb to wonder, rarely considering the fact that each of us is unique in all of space and all of time. We become forgetful, even of our own existence. Here is a possibility to be realized: Through the active consideration of transforming ourselves, of becoming consciously involved in our own evolution, we can reawaken to the miracle of existence. Through simple strategies and patient, diligent practice, we can reclaim the feeling of wonder we held so carelessly between our hands on summer days when we were very young.

# The ITP Kata:
# The Tao of Practice

As noted earlier, the Japanese word *kata* (kah-tah) means "form." Our usage here is similar to that in the martial arts, where the practitioner performs a series of predetermined moves. The ITP Kata was designed by George Leonard to be performed in forty minutes, each element blending into the next without a sense of haste. You can trace its lineage to hatha yoga, the martial arts, modern exercise physiology, Progressive Relaxation, visualization research, and witness meditation. It offers practitioners the following benefits:

Balances and centers the body and psyche

Provides a generalized warm-up, speeding the heartbeat, increasing the flow of blood and sending an infusion of heat to all parts of the body

Articulates practically every joint in the body, enhancing the lubrication of the synovial joints (those such as the shoulder or knee, which are surrounded by capsules filled with synovial fluid)

Makes available a comprehensive course of stretches, increasing flexibility in all major muscle groups

Includes three essential strength exercises

Provides a full set of Progressive Relaxation exercises, in which muscle groups are tightened then allowed to relax deeply

Presents numerous opportunities for deep, rhythmic breathing

Includes a period devoted to transformational imaging during which the powers of intentionality can be applied to making positive changes in body and psyche

Concludes with ten minutes of meditation

While the ITP Kata can be performed in forty minutes without hurrying, parts of it may be extended for as long as the practitioner desires. This is especially true of the last two sections (transformational imaging and meditation). Participants in our experimental classes committed themselves to doing the Kata at least five times a week, and we consider this one of the commitments for full participation in the Integral Transformative Practice program. Many practitioners have found it best to do the Kata in the morning for the relaxing, centering, and energizing effect it would have on their whole day.

The ITP Kata embodies the definition of practice itself; that is, an activity that, *for all its benefits*, is done on a regular basis primarily for its own sake, because it is the path upon which you walk. The Kata can be practiced in a group or alone. Group practice gathers power from sharing rhythm and intentionality with others. But even when practicing in solitude, you can be reasonably sure that other people are going through the same sequence of movements and experiences, thus creating a community, whether visible or invisible.

Like many of our participants, you might at first find it a bit frustrating to learn some of the movements and perform them in such a way that they flow smoothly, one into the other. But this practice does not demand the skill of a martial artist or dancer; most people achieve a degree of proficiency after only a few sessions. A few weeks after starting to do the Kata, you, like some of our participants, might encounter a reluctance to continue your practice. This is perfectly natural, a manifestation of the resistance to any significant change in your life, whether for ill or for good, the homeostasis that we have discussed in chapter 3. But if you simply persist, you will in all likelihood arrive at the day when it is easier to do the Kata than not to do it. That, in any case, has been the experience of most of our participants. At the end of our first year's training, participants filled out evaluation forms. The two first items were: "(1) Rank the following ITP elements in order of importance in enhancing your ITP practice," and "(2) Rank the same ITP elements as to their value in your life." All the major elements of the ITP practice were listed. In both cases, participants ranked the Kata second, just below affirmations.

You'll need no special equipment to do the ITP Kata, only a carpeted floor or mat and loose clothing or perhaps an outdoor setting, a soft surface covered with a blanket or mat. Start slowly and use common sense. Don't push any of the stretches to the point of strain or pain. If any exercise seems too strenuous, do it easily at first or even partially. For guidance, tune into your own sensations and feelings. In performing the Kata, think in terms of months or years, not days or weeks. To shift from short-term to long-term thinking and acting is to gain what might well be the most important lesson this training has to offer. An outline of the ITP Kata is presented below, followed by detailed descriptions of each step, with illustrations where needed.

## BALANCE AND CENTER—GRACE

**The ITP Kata, Step by Step**

The word GRACE serves here as an acronym, a sort of pilot's check list for balancing and centering. Start in an upright stance, without shoes, feet shoulder-width apart, eyes open and soft. Spend a few seconds on each letter of the word:

*G—Ground* Imagine what it would be like if your feet and legs extended down through the surface beneath you and deep into the earth. Feel your weight shifting downward. Let your knees bend ever so slightly. Be aware of the loving embrace of gravity. Consider your profound connection with this planet and, through that, your connection with the entire universe.

*R—Relax* Breathe deeply. Exhale all the way. Let all your face muscles relax completely. Feel your shoulders melting downward. Release

## THE ITP KATA IN OUTLINE

Balance and Center—GRACE

The Water Series
1. Drill for water, 4 left, 4 right
2. Pump water, 6
3. Fountain, 6
4. Finger spray, 4
5. Half windmill, 4 (left, right, left, right)
6. Rowing, 10 left, 10 right, with reach and shake

Articulation
7. Shoulder rotation, 4 forward, 4 back
8. Head rotation, 4 each of 3 variations
9. Arm swing, 12
10. Pelvic rotation, 4 left, 4 right
11. Knee rotation, 4 left, 4 right

Floor Series
12. Hip joint rotation, 8
13. Quad tightening, 6 x 6"
14. Foot rotation, 4 counterclockwise, 4 clockwise
15. Hamstring stretch
16. Hip stretch
17. Quad stretch
18. Back stretch
19. Spinal curl
20. Curl-up, 5 x 10"
21. Elongation stretch, 2
22. Groin stretch

Mini Yoga
23. Sun salutation, 2
24. Spinal twist (left & right)
25. Deep relaxation

Transformational Imaging

Ten-Minute Meditation

the tension in your chest, your abdomen, your back, your pelvic area, your legs. Feel a warming, melting sensation moving down your entire body, your hands becoming warm and heavy, the soles of your feet warming the surface beneath them and that surface warming the soles of your feet.

*A—Aware* Let yourself become keenly aware of your surroundings: the objects in the enclosed space you are inhabiting, the outdoor world you can see through the window—the condition of the sky, the wind moving the leaves, the infusion of light. Sense the air that caresses every inch of your body. Let there be eyes all over you, in your back as well as front—the small of your back, the back of your neck, the back of your knees. Tune in to every sound and every smell and also to every sensation that has no commonly accepted name. Let all that you can sense become a part of you. What would it be like if a stone owned some measure of consciousness? Affirm your kinship with the material world. Consider the possibility of other, coexistent worlds now invisible to your senses.

*C—Center* Touch your abdomen about an inch below your navel. Here, in the center of your belly, is the body's center of mass. By focusing your attention on this point, whether in stillness or in motion, you can achieve the calmness that empowers and the power that contributes to good in the world. Breathe deeply, letting your abdomen expand. Ask yourself this question: "Am I willing to get in touch with and use my own best and truest power?"

*E—Energize* Hold your arms open in front of you with your hands wide open. Imagine energy—high voltage electricity, for example— shooting from your outspread fingertips. With knees slightly bent, shift your body around, sensing this energy inhabiting every part of you. Check to see if this energy is equal and even—right and left, back and front, top and bottom. Move around the room in this energized, balanced, centered, relaxed state. Then return to your original position.

**The Water Series**

### 1. DRILL FOR WATER

Place your feet wider apart—separated by about two feet. Imagine a wheel mounted horizontally directly in front of you. Its diameter is the same as the space between your feet, and it has a crank handle on top near the edge. Grasp this imaginary handle with both hands and begin turning the wheel, as if you were drilling for water deep in the earth. Bend your knees and shift your body from side to side as you drill. Keep your trunk upright. Don't bend your upper body. The side to side motion is accomplished entirely by your legs. Keep your feet in full contact with the surface beneath you, as if they were sinking into it. Turn the large wheel counterclockwise four times, then clockwise four times. Breathe deeply during this exercise. Become aware of your heart beginning to beat faster. Proceed directly and smoothly into the next exercise.

### 2. PUMP WATER

Continue to stand with feet apart. Clasp your hands in front of you and raise them above your head, taking in a very large breath as you do so. Lean back slightly and look up at your hands. Then let grav-

*1. Drill for water*          *2. Pump water*

ity take your upper body forward and into a deep bend, so that your hands are between your legs, exhaling heartily with this pumping motion. It's important to leave your knees bent and to be gentle with your lower back during the next movement, in which you uncurl your upper body, bringing it to the previous upright, leaned-back position. As in all of these exercises, keep your feet firmly connected to the floor surface; don't let your toes or heels rise. After six full pumping motions, go directly into the next exercise, continuing the rhythmic breathing. If you're having trouble with your lower back, skip this exercise.

### 3 · Fountain

Exhaling strongly, reach straight down as if to scoop up a large amount of water, bringing your hands together just in front of your feet. Bend your knees as much as you can without strain as you reach down. Don't overdo it. Bear in mind that this can be a strenuous exercise. Start rising toward an upright position, inhaling deeply. Bring the backs of your hands together as they pass your chest on the way up, then rotate them so that the palms are pressed together as they

*3. Fountain*

pass your face, then so that the backs are again touching as they reach high above your head. All this occurs in a smooth, continuous motion. Swing your hands out to the sides and down, making an imaginary fountain as you once again reach down to scoop up water, exhaling as you do so. Reach down six times. On the last repetition, stop your arms' downward motion when they are straight out to the sides, and go directly into the next exercise.

### 4. Finger Spray

With hands extended straight out to the sides, clench and unclench your fist, as if spraying water from the tips of your fingers. Do this rather slowly four times, attending to the articulation of all ten fingers.

### 5. Half Windmill

Place your right hand on your hip. Bring your left hand out to the side, watching it swing up over your head and down in a wide arc to

*4. Finger spray*                    *5. Half windmill*

the right of your body, bending your upper body to the right as you do so. Inhale as your hand rises and exhale as it descends. Reverse the positions of the hands, this time bending to the left, for a total of four repetitions.

### 6. Rowing

Place the toe of your left foot about fifteen inches behind the heel of your right foot and turn the left foot out at a forty-five-degree angle as you prepare to rock steadily forward and back with your entire lower body. As you rock forward, your right knee should bend slightly as the left leg straightens. When you rock back, the right leg straightens as the left leg bends. The upper body stays upright or *slightly* forward during the entire exercise. Both feet remain firmly on the ground.

Curl your fingers into a loose fist, with the backs of your hands forward. As you rock forward, swing your arms forward. As you rock back, return your arms to your sides.

*6. Rowing*

Check your balance. If you find yourself unbalanced in any way, forward or back, left or right, make the necessary adjustments. As you continue this rowing motion, focus awareness on your center. Let your center initiate and lead each motion. Have it be the source of a deep, soft power like that of a wave moving onto the beach, then subsiding.

After you have completed ten forward and back motions with the right foot forward, bring the left foot forward to the usual side-by-side stance. With a large incoming breath, reach high above your head with both hands as if to cup a piece of the sky in your hands. Bring your gently clasped hands down to your center while exhaling and shake your clasped hands so vigorously that you vibrate all over. Let this vibration shake any tension out of your body.

Now release your hands and repeat the rowing exercise ten times with your left foot forward, followed by another reach and shake.

**Articulation**                7. SHOULDER ROTATION

With your arms hanging by your sides, roll your shoulders forward four times, then backward four times. Keep your hands alive and energized while doing so.

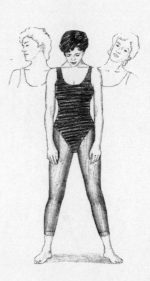

*7. Shoulder rotation*          *8. Head rotation*

## 8. HEAD ROTATION

Turn your head left, then right for a total of four stretches. Then tilt your head first left, then right, as if trying to touch ears to shoulders, for four stretches. Continue by bringing chin to chest, then back to the upright position for four stretches. These exercises should be done carefully and consciously. Sense the articulation of the cervical vertebrae *from the inside*. Make no sudden or extreme movements. Don't try to tilt your head far back.

## 9. ARM SWING

Standing upright with feet planted firmly in a wide stance, begin a vigorous rotary movement, turning hips, trunk, and head first right, then left. Let your arms hang as limp as pieces of wet spaghetti during this exercise. Centrifugal force will cause them to swing out during rotation and slap against your body when you start to turn the other way. Let your shoulders relax. Be aware of your center. Make sure your feet don't rise from the ground. Do a total of twelve moves.

*9. Arm swing*

### 10. Pelvic Rotation

Maintaining a deeply rooted wide stance, place your hands on your hips, bend your knees, and, in the manner of a belly dancer, rotate your pelvic area in a strong horizontal circle, four times left, then four times right.

### 11. Knee Rotation

Bring your feet together. With the palms of both hands, gently hold your knees together while rotating them in a horizontal circle to the left. Try to keep your feet flat on the floor during this movement, thus articulating the ankle joints. After four rotations to the left, press your knees gently back. Complete the execise with four rotations to the right. Again press the knees back.

**The Floor Series**

### 12. Hip Joint Rotation

Sit on the floor with your legs extended in front of you, your feet about eighteen inches apart. Support your upper body with your arms if need be. Turn your feet out as far as possible, then in as far as possible for a total of eight moves. Feel the rotation in your hip joints.

10. *Pelvic rotation*      11. *Knee rotation*      12. *Hip joint rotation*

### 13. Quad Tightening

Continue sitting on the floor with legs extended straight in front of you and feet together. Now take a deep breath and press your knees down as hard as you can for six seconds. Then totally relax, exhaling fully. Repeat six times, pressing your knees down *into* the surface beneath them. In this, as in all other exercises that stress the muscles, put full attention on the relaxation phase as well as on the stress phase.

### 14. Foot Rotation

Lie on your back and draw your knees up with feet flat on the floor. Lift your left leg and grasp it beneath the knee with both hands. Rotate your left foot four times counterclockwise and four times clockwise, moving your toes as you do so. Continue working with your left leg for the next three exercises.

### 15. Hamstring Stretch

Still lying on your back with knees up and feet flat on the floor, lift your left leg, straighten it completely, grasp it beneath the knee with both hands and draw it back as far as you can without pain. Some very flexible people will be able to draw it back far enough to grasp the foot or ankle, but the important thing is keeping the leg straight at the knee rather than seeing how far back you can draw it. Hold this stretch for twenty seconds. Go directly into the next exercise. The next period for relaxation comes after the quad stretch (#17).

*13. Quad tightening*          *14. Foot rotation*          *15. Hamstring stretch*

### 16. HIP STRETCH

Begin again lying on your back with knees up and feet flat on the floor. Cross your right ankle over your left leg. Lift the left leg and grasp it beneath the knee, drawing it back so as to put a rotary stretch on your right hip joint. Hold for twelve seconds. Move directly into the next exercise.

### 17. QUAD STRETCH

Roll over on your right side. Reach down behind you, grasp your left ankle with your left hand and pull it toward your buttocks. This will stretch your left quadriceps, the muscles on the front of your upper leg. (You can use your right hand to cradle your head.) Hold the stretch for twelve seconds. Relax fully.

Now go back to *Foot Rotation* and repeat exercises 14 through 17 with your right leg. Again relax.

### 18. BACK STRETCH

Lying on your back, draw the knees up, slide both arms beneath them and hug them to you, lifting your head so it comes down to or even in between the knees. Hold this stretch for sixteen seconds.

*16. Hip stretch*

*17. Quad stretch*

*18. Back stretch*

### 19. Spinal Curl

Leave your knees up, feet flat on the floor, hands palms down a few inches out from your sides. Start curling your pelvis up, lifting the tailbone off the floor. Inhaling while you do so, lift each vertebra off the floor, one after the other, starting with the lowest, until you are balanced on your feet, head, shoulder blades, and arms. Tighten your buttocks and hold for a count of twelve. Exhaling, lower your vertebrae to the floor, one after the other, in reverse order, then relax.

### 20. Curl-up

Lie on your back, knees drawn up, feet flat on the floor. If you haven't done much in the way of abdominal exercises, cross your arms over your lower chest. If your abdomen is already toned to some extent, grasp the back of your right hand with your left hand and place the back of your left hand on your forehead. Now suck in your abdomen and press the small of your back down tight against the floor, bringing your pubic bone as close to your lower ribs as you can. Then inhale and gently curl up your head and shoulders until your shoulder blades come up off the floor, and maybe a little higher. Hold for a count of ten, then slowly lower your shoulders and head to the floor while exhaling. As an alternative, you can pulse upward slightly ten times in rhythm with your count before lowering shoulders and head.

It's most important to keep the small of your back against the floor throughout the exercise. If the back should begin to arch, it means you're tiring and should stop.

*19. Spinal curl*              *20. Curl-up*

This exercise is very important since it strengthens the muscles that function as back stabilizers. Be sure to start slowly. Repeat for a total of five times. If you can do so without feeling significant muscular effort, it probably means you aren't doing the exercise right. Try raising your upper body a little higher off the floor.

### 21. ELONGATION STRETCH

Take a few moments to relax. Then stretch both arms out along the floor above your head. Take a deep breath and try to lengthen your body, extending your hands and arms in one direction and your feet and legs in the opposite direction. Open your mouth wide and yawn if you wish. Then relax completely. Inhale and stretch again, and this time, as you exhale, curl up into a sitting position and go straight into the next exercise. (If you're having back problems, don't try to curl straight up. Instead, turn on your side and use your arms and hands to help you rise to a sitting position. Remember to use common sense and take care of your own particular needs on all these exercises.)

### 22. GROIN STRETCH

From a sitting position, grasp your ankles and draw them back as close to your groin as you comfortably can, pressing the soles of your feet together. Lean forward and press your knees toward the floor with your elbows. Hold the stretch for twelve seconds. Then gently release the stretch and come to a standing position for the next exercise.

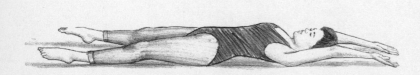

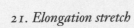

*21. Elongation stretch*

*22. Groin stretch*

23. SUN SALUTATION                                      **Mini Yoga**

Yoga is among the most ancient of tranformative practices, with roots perhaps in Stone Age shamanism. The word itself comes from the Sanskrit "yoke," meaning to bring together, to make whole. Yoga is not a religion but a means for making one whole. The physical aspect of yogic practice that involves stretches and postures is called hatha yoga and is unsurpassed in balancing the muscle groups; if you stretch forward, for example, you'll also stretch backward.

The sun salutation is a sort of yoga anthology, putting together a coherent series of essential yogic postures. It is best performed not by rote but with full consciousness as a salute to the sun, to nature, to the strange and wondrous universe in which we live.

1. Stand tall with feet together and inhale deeply, expanding first the lower abdomen, then the lower chest, then the upper chest. Exhale, then press your palms together in front of your chest, touching the area of the heart with the back of your thumbs.

2. Inhale. Lock your thumbs and extend your hands out in front of you. Watch your hands as you raise them high above your head. With knees slightly bent, lean backward from your hips as far as is comfortable.

3. Exhale and fold slowly forward from your waist until your hands are on the floor just outside your feet. If necessary bend your knees.

4. Inhale. Leaving your right foot between your hands, extend your left foot far back and place your left knee on the floor. Bring your right knee up to your chest and look up.

5. Exhale and extend your right foot back to meet the left, leaving your hands where they are. Push your buttocks up to make a triangle with the floor. Look at your feet and lower your heels toward the floor.

6. Begin to inhale. Lower your knees, chest, and chin to the floor, leaving your pelvis raised. Keep your palms beneath your shoulders, your elbows in close to your body.

7. Continue to inhale. Lower your pelvis to the floor and let your head and shoulder curl upward like a cobra ready to strike. Look up.

8. Exhale and push yourself up in the triangle again as in posture five.

9. Inhale and swing your left foot forward between your hands. This leaves your right foot stretched back with the right knee on the floor. Your left knee is up against your chest. Look up as in posture four.

10. Exhale. Swing your right foot forward until it is next to the left foot between your hands. Straighten your knees while keeping your arms and hands down, on or near the floor. Don't strain.

11. Inhale. Lock your thumbs and unfold your body slowly and consciously to a standing position. Look up at your hands as you keep bending backward as far as is comfortable.

12. Exhale. Slowly and consciously bring your palms together in front of your chest, the backs of the thumbs touching the heart area.

Put your feet about shoulder-width apart, take a deep breath, and relax for a moment before repeating the sun salutation exercise. Then lie flat on your back in the relaxation position—eyes closed, feet about shoulder-width apart, hands out a few inches from your sides, palms up—and become aware of your heartbeat slowing.

#1          #2          #3          #4

23. Sun salutation

#5

#6

#7

#8

*23. Sun salutation (cont.)*

#9

#10

#11

#12

### 24. SPINAL TWIST

Lying on your back, extend your arms straight out to the sides, palms up. Draw your knees up, feet flat on the floor, and take a deep breath. Cross your right leg over the left and let both knees swing to the right, turning your head and upper body toward the left as you exhale. Hold this position for twelve seconds, then reverse the procedure.

### 25. DEEP RELAXATION

Before beginning, make sure you're comfortably and warmly dressed and that no bright lights are shining in your eyes. For the first few times, it would be best to have someone read the following instructions aloud in a clear, soothing voice, pausing where there are three dots. You might record the instructions, then play them back or listen to George Leonard's voice on the *Tao of Practice* videotape. (For information on ordering a videotape of the ITP Kata, see Appendix A.)

"Lie comfortably on your back in the relaxation position, eyes closed. Become aware of the rhythmic rise and fall of your chest and abdomen as you breathe. Let the floor support you.... In the next series of exercises, you'll be tensing then relaxing certain muscles. When tensing a particular muscle, do the best you can to leave the rest of your body completely relaxed. In some of these exercises you'll be lifting your legs or arms a few inches off the floor as you tense them. When you hear the signal to let them drop, release them completely, as if a string has been cut from a puppet. You'll be exhaling on each relaxation....

"Start by focusing your awareness on the center of your abdo-

*24. Spinal twist*

men. . . . Now let your awareness travel down to your right leg. Extend it out along the floor. Take a deep breath and lift your leg a few inches off the floor, tightening its muscles from the toes to the hip. Hold it. Hold it. . . . Exhale and let it drop. Roll your leg gently from side to side and relax it. . . . Now send your awareness to your left leg. Extend it out along the floor. Take a deep breath and lift it a few inches, tensing all its muscles from the toes to the hip. . . . Tight, tight, tight. . . . Let it drop. Roll it gently from side to side and relax it completely. . . .

"Awareness on your right arm and hand. Extend your arm out along the floor, tensing the muscles. Splay out the fingers, take a deep breath, make a fist, and raise your arm a few inches off the floor, tightening it all the way up to the shoulders. . . . Hold it. Tight, tight. . . . Let it drop. Roll it gently from side to side and relax your arm and hand completely. . . . Awareness on your left arm and hand. Extend your left arm out along the floor, tensing the muscles. Splay out the fingers, take a deep breath, make a fist, and raise your arm a few inches off the floor, tightening it all the way up to the shoulders. . . . Hold it. Tight, tight. . . . Let it drop. Roll it gently from side to side and relax your arm and hand completely. . . .

"Awareness now to your pelvis and buttocks. Take a deep breath and tighten your pelvis and buttocks. . . . Hold it a little longer. . . . Exhale and relax your pelvis and buttocks completely. Roll your lower body gently from side to side and relax completely. . . .

"Now with a big incoming breath, puff up your abdomen like a large balloon. . . . Make it a little larger. . . . Open your mouth and let the air *rush* out. . . .

"With an even larger incoming breath, puff up your chest like an even larger balloon. . . . Larger. . . . Open your mouth and let the air *rush* out. . . .

"Awareness to your shoulders. With a deep inhalation, raise and tighten your shoulders. Curl them foward, as if around your chest. Pull them far back, hard against the floor. . . . Release your breath and relax your shoulders completely, working them down toward your feet. . . .

"Roll your head gently from side to side. . . . Bringing your head to the center, relax your neck and throat completely. . . .

"Open your mouth wide. Take in a big breath. Move your jaw around, releasing all the tension. Yawn if you wish. . . . Relax your mouth and jaw completely. . . .

"Puff out your cheeks.... Suck in your cheeks.... Relax your cheeks.

"Tighten your face. Make it tiny. Squeeze all the facial muscles together. Bring everything in close to your nose.... Relax your face. Feel all the muscles in your face relaxing completely....

"Raise your eyebrows and wrinkle your forehead.... Relax your eyebrows and forehead....

"Now we're going to take an interior journey through your body, relaxing any subtle tensions without moving. We'll start the journey by focusing awareness on your center. Let that awareness move down to your legs, your feet, your toes. Relax your big toes, your second toes, your third, fourth, and fifth toes. . . . Relax the soles of your feet and the tops of your feet. Relax your ankles, your lower legs, and your upper legs.... Let your awareness now turn to your arms, hands, and fingers. Relax your thumbs, your index fingers, your third, fourth and fifth fingers. Relax the palms of your hands and the backs of your hands.... Relax your wrists, your lower arms, and your upper arms. Relax your shoulders. Let the tension melt away.... Awareness now to your buttocks and pelvis. Relax completely. Let all the tension melt away.... And now your abdomen. Relax all the muscles and all the organs of your abdomen.... Relax your diaphram. Relax your chest, your heart, your lungs.... Once again, relax your shoulders. Relax them completely, from the inside.... Relax your lower back, your middle back, your upper back. Relax your throat, your jaw, your tongue. Relax your cheeks, your temples, your ears, your eyes, your eyelids. Relax your forehead, your scalp, the back of your neck.... Relax all your body. Become a pure witness. Experience your body in complete relaxation.... Now become aware of your breath as it flows in and flows out with no effort on your part. Don't try to control it. Just witness it.... Become aware of any thoughts that might be floating through your mind. Just observe them.... Now take this opportunity to become aware of the peace and joy of existence itelf, the invisible connections that join us with all beings, with all of the universe, with the miracle of the life we are given."

At this point, you're ready for the final two stages of the ITP Kata: Transformational Imaging and Induction and Witness Meditation. A separate chapter will be devoted to each of these.

# SEVEN

# The ITP Kata: Transformational Imaging

In this section of the Kata, we use mental imagery to foster positive changes of body, mind, heart, and soul. This practice gives you a chance to strengthen your affirmations, but you need not limit yourself. Here you can work to improve *any* aspect of your physical and psychological functioning. Before describing this set of exercises, though, we will say a few words about the transformative power of mental images.

All of us have experienced the influence of imagery upon our body, emotions, and impulses. If, for example, we constantly see ourself losing a game, we are more likely to lose that game than we would be if we had a positive attitude toward it. If we habitually dwell upon people's shortcomings, we are less likely to respect them than we would be if we focused on their virtues and strengths. If we carry a persistent image that we have some undiscovered disease, we will probably dampen our mood and might even depress our immune system.

This is not a new insight. It has long been thought that powerful pictures in the mind produce lasting changes of psyche and soma. Doctors of Greek and Roman antiquity, for example, believed that images and feelings actually moved in the blood, directly affecting emotions and physical functioning. According to a famous Hippocratic maxim, imagination and bodily processes "tread in a ring," constantly influencing one another. This belief was generally held in Europe until the late seventeenth century. One Renaissance doctor, for example, wrote that imagination "marks and deformes, nay, sometimes kills Embryos in the womb, hastens Births, or causes Abortions." In *Approved Directions for Health* (1612), William Vaughan declared that the physician "must invent and devise some spiritual pageant to fortify and help the imaginative faculty, which is corrupted and depraved; yea, he must endeavor to deceive and imprint another conceit, whether it be wise or foolish, in the patient's braine, thereby to put out all former phantasies." These words reflect the general opinion of the day that mental process is profoundly connected with bodily process.

Eastern cultures hold a similar view. India's Ayurvedic medicine advocates spiritual practices—as well as herbal and other physical agencies—to improve one's psychological and physical functioning. Chinese healing practice, which was deeply influenced by the integral worldview of Taoist yoga, enlists the mind in its approach to health. In both China and India, for more than two thousand years, philosophers and healers have viewed human nature as a single hierarchical structure in which mind and body are profoundly joined.

From the late 1600s until recent decades, however, this holistic understanding was largely displaced in the West. The French philosopher René Descartes argued that mind and body operate on parallel tracks, in different domains of existence, so that mind "has no need of place, and is not dependent on any material thing." This view came to dominate Western science and supported the mechanistic medicine of the eighteenth and nineteenth centuries (which was influenced by the discovery that much of our somatic functioning can be understood in terms of hydraulics and engineering principles). The study of human nature was compartmentalized, the body being assigned to anatomists and physiologists, the mind to philosophers and psychologists. The unified psychophysiology of ancient Greece, the Renaissance, and Eastern cultures was replaced by a science that separated psychological from somatic sickness. This attitude led many physicians and lay people to devalue the mind's role in healing and contributed to psychologists' neglect of imagery's transformative power.

But things change. In the twentieth century, and especially since the 1960s, researchers have discovered new links between mind and the flesh and are returning to a holistic view of human nature. Imagery has become a legitimate object of study by experimental psychologists and is used with increasing frequency by psychotherapists, sport psychologists, and others to foster healing, performance, and growth. The view that mind and body form an integral entity is respectable among scientists again. Indeed, many connections between the two are understood better than ever.

Laboratory tests have shown, for example, that the immune system can be strengthened (or weakened) by images, attitudes, and emotions. Many agencies of such influence have been identified, among them molecules called opioid peptides secreted by the brain and other organs that attach to specific receptor sites throughout the body. Numerous studies have shown that these molecules cause alterations of mood, pain, and pleasure and that they influence the immune system. The immune system in turn affects the nervous system through glandular secretions. Many *two-way* paths among the nervous, endocrine, and immune systems have been discovered, and it has been shown that all of these can be directly affected by our thoughts and feelings. The cumulative results of such research confirm the ancient belief that mind and body constantly interact, influencing each other for better or worse. Greek, Indian, Chinese, and Renaissance doctors were right when they said that thoughts are intimately involved with feelings and the flesh.

As the study of imagery's power develops, researchers are increasingly impressed with its specificity. It has been shown, for example, that elaborate marks, which appear spontaneously on the bodies of certain people, dramatize signficant emotional issues. These marks, sometimes called "hysterical stigmata," are caused in large part by a vivid mental process. For instance, a woman described in the British medical journal *Lancet* by physician Robert Moody exhibited a bruise that resembled an elaborately carved death's head on a walking stick her father had used to beat her. This bruise, according to Moody, arose spontaneously, without external manipulation, during a psychotherapy session. The huge number of cells and the complexity of physiological processes involved in such marks have caused researchers to marvel at the body's capacity for specific alteration and its responsiveness to highly charged imagery.

The effects of placebos also dramatize the exactitude with which mind can affect the body. Studies at hospitals, medical schools, and drug companies show that dummy treatments such as sugar pills relieve many kinds of affliction, produce toxic side effects (when they are expected to), and catalyze dramatic changes of mood and behavior. The alterations produced by placebos, which in themselves have no specific effects, have convinced medical people that human beings can alter their functioning without external devices. Even though they are inert substances or nothing more than sugar pills, placebos have been used to relieve angina pectoris, allergies, seasickness, anxiety, postoperative pain, warts, asthma, arthritis, depression, sleep disorders, obesity, and many other afflictions. Dummy treatments have caused intoxication, euphoria, blurred vision, dizziness, increased libido, lumbar pain, heart palpitations, and serenity among people who expected such reactions. Expectations of particular results, in conjunction with accompanying rehearsals of them (which may be unconscious), produce the expected outcomes.

Consider the implications of these placebo effects. If, for example, they produce relief from allergies—which can be highly resistant to standard therapies—what does this tell us about the powers of mind in the body? Allergies involve interactions among trillions of cells and virtually all of the body's organs; getting rid of them requires precise alterations of the nervous, hormonal, and immune systems. That men and women do in fact get rid of them simply because they believe in a sugar pill has caused medical people to marvel at our abilities for self-transformation. Placebo effects have forced researchers to see that the mind can touch *just the right tissues* and shift the functioning of *just the right cells* involved in the change, rebalancing the body all the while as it breaks its familiar patterns. Indeed, to relieve an allergy through mental imagery can be considered a supreme athletic feat. Such feats suggest that we harbor possibilities for change that we have hardly tapped yet.

Well-established scientific research on placebo effects, hysterical stigmata, and other prodigies of psychosomatic change show that sustained mental imagery can induce positive (as well as negative) alterations of thought, feeling, and the flesh. In the sections that follow, we give specific instructions for the use of such imagery to foster creative changes of body, mind, heart, and soul.

Back to the ITP Kata. You've just finished a session of deep relaxation. You're lying on your back, feet shoulder-width apart, hands on the floor a few inches from your sides, palms up. Inhaling deeply, swing your arms out from your sides and around in a wide arc until they are above your head on the floor. Exhaling, bring your hands from above your head down the front of your body, palms toward your feet, as if you are pushing a wave of energy from above your head all the way past your feet. Your hands don't touch your body; with practice, however, you'll probably learn to feel what might be called an energy wave, not just on the front of your body but all the way through it. As you create each wave, you might say, "My entire being is balanced, vital, and healthy," silently or aloud. You can use any affirmation you wish with this exercise, or none at all. The basic idea here is overall health, vitality, and balance.

**Imaging in the Kata**

After creating several waves, you can move on to any part of your body you wish, using imaging (as will be described in the examples below) as an aid to provide preventive maintenance, repair defective functioning, or produce positive bodily changes ranging from what is considered normal to what would be considered extraordinary. Feel free to include any positive bodily changes you desire.

We recommend that, as is the case with affirmations, you employ positive statements expressed in the present tense for whatever words you use in helping create your images. This is by no means to deny the reality of any undesirable or unwanted prevailing condition. Yes, the undesirable condition does exist in the material realm. Your job is to bring the condition that you intend to realize into sharp, positive, present-tense focus in your consciousness.

What if you are a person who doesn't easily create images? Do the exercises anyway. Keep practicing. Don't expect immediate results; you're in this practice for the long term. And don't be discouraged if your image lacks clarity and sharp focus. Even a glimmering of yourself as you wish to be can bring effective results. Still, you may be surprised to find that your imaging ability improves with practice. Also bear in mind that images don't have to be visual. Some people tend to create kinesthetic images, feeling images, which can be powerful and effective. You might well be able to *feel* the way it would be if you had, say, a relaxed, supple, erect posture. Some people have auditory imagery. Others have images of smell and taste.

But a word of caution: In the healing funtion, Integral Transformative Practice is not meant to supplant mainstream medical science. An integral practice is not exclusive; it reaches out to the best of all that is available. Our medical science has developed many effective techniques, especially in diagnosis, the treatment of trauma and infection, and the development of life support technology. Members of our ITP groups were urged to use good judgment and common sense in dealing with undesirable bodily conditions, to use ITP if need be as a *complement* to mainstream, Eastern, or alternative methods. In many cases, ITP seemed greatly to enhance the effects of mainstream medical treatments already underway. Bear in mind that any decision to transform body, mind, spirit, or heart is your responsibility.

Here are a few sample exercises for this section of the Kata. Unless otherwise noted, all are done while lying down. Note that in this practice every imaging exercise invokes the body, whether or not you are imaging a purely physical transformation. Our experience has shown that by somehow grounding every image in the marvelous physical entity we call a body, we significantly increase the effectiveness of the exercise. We also recommend that you take a moment after each imaging exercise to lie still in an attitude of acceptance, thankfulness, and alignment with God or the universe.

*To help improve vision.* Rub your hands together briskly until the palms are warm. Cup your palms over your closed eyes to exclude all light and let your eyes relax completely. Take a few moments to gently massage your closed eyes with the pads of your fingers. Then cup your hands a few inches *above* your closed eyes and begin a stroking or massaging motion, as if the heat or other energy from your hands is somehow moving or otherwise affecting not only the suface but also the interior of the eyes. If at first you don't feel any effect in the eyes themselves—a sort of warmth, pressure, "magnetism," or presence—simply continue the exercise. Chances are you'll feel it after a few days' practice.

At the same time, begin to create a vivid mental image of your eyes as totally healthy and your vision as extremely sharp. Mentally,

*The galaxies exist in you, not printed as mere images within your skull, but in your every cell, your every atom.*

G.L.

see the visible world as bright, sparkling, and crystal clear. If you're imaging not just normal but metanormal telescopic vision, create an image of a small bird in a distant tree. Note the color of its plumage, the precise shape of its bill, the sharp lines that delineate its eyes. Track the bird as it flits from one branch to another. See if you can pick out individual feathers.

If you wish to use words with mental images and the stroking motion of your hands, here are some samples: "My vision is crystal clear and my eyes are balanced, vital, and healthy." "The lenses of my eyes are clear, perfectly shaped, and completely healthy." "The aqueous fluid in my lenses is pure and clear and circulating healthily." In every case, use words that feel right to you. Go with the ones that touch your heart.

***To help prevent or reverse coronary artery disease.*** Rub your hands vigorously together. Place your left hand on your heart and your right hand on your left hand. Physically massage your heart area with a feeling of love and caring for your heart. Slide your right hand down to your *hara* or physical center, about an inch or so below your navel; leave it there as a strong connection between your center of feeling (the heart) and your center of action and intuition (the *hara*). Lift your left hand a few inches above your body and begin a stroking motion with the intentionality of "touching" your physical heart. With practice, just as in the case of your eyes, you'll probably be able to feel the sensation of your hand's energy in your heart itself.

Aware now of your heart's approximate shape and size, begin to image it as balanced, vital, healthy, and fully alive with radiant energy. "My entire heart is balanced, vital, and healthy." "My heart is pulsing in perfect rhythm." Then image or "feel" your heart's arteries. (If you wish, use a picture from an anatomy book as a model for your image.) Begin to create an image of your arteries as open, supple, and healthy. Repeat those words if you so desire while continuing the stroking motion of your left hand: "My heart's arteries are open, supple, and healthy." Use any words that feel right for you or no words at all, just a sharp, clear visual or feeling image of your coronary arteries as strongly pumping life-giving blood to all areas of your heart.

Slide your right hand up over your heart area and your left hand down to your belly. Repeat the above induction, this time reversing the two hands' roles. Be sure to "feel" all of the heart, including the top, bottom, and back, and all the arteries.

***To help open your heart to others, to be a more loving person.*** Bring your left hand to your heart center and place your right hand over the left. Ask yourself, "What would it be like if I were a more loving person?" Begin to create an image of yourself as open-hearted and loving, a person who experiences deep compassion for others. Imagine meeting a person with whom you have been less than compassionate and loving. Bring an image of this person to your mind. Create a vivid mental and emotional experience of opening your heart to her or him. Tune in to the present-tense feelings in your body as you do so. How does your body feel when you approach someone in this open-hearted manner? What are the particular qualities of the feeling? Explore different images. Try taking a deep breath and physically opening your arms wide, expanding your rib cage, making your heart available to others. Stay with it. Pick a vision that brings a thrill to your body, a feeling of the many possibilities that open up when you open your heart to someone previously unloved. Expand this feeling to encompass all of humanity.

***To help reshape your body.*** Start by focusing strongly on the part of your physical body you want to change. Stroke your hands over it, increasing the awareness in that part. Bear in mind that energy follows attention. Sense the additional energy now localized in the body part given extra attention. Let's say you want to reduce your waistline. Here you might follow the example of the ITP practitioner who reduced his waist measurements by two inches in three months by imagining a "girdle of fire" around his middle (see chapter 4). In his case, the image became vivid in his consciousness not just while doing the Kata but during many of his waking hours. Successful transformation is almost always closely related to the practitioner's ability to produce and hold a vivid, positive, present-tense image—then, at times, to surrender to grace. It's also important that you choose an imaging and induction procedure that's right for you, one that expresses your own personal being.

***To help improve physical performance.*** Say your best time for a 10K race is forty-two minutes, and you've made an affirmation to run that distance in thirty-eight minutes. Place your right hand over your *hara* and your left hand over your right hand. Now bring to mind the race itself. Make everything vivid and present: the wind on your face as you're warming up, the tingling, fully alive feeling that goes along with removing your warm-up garb and standing at the starting line, the exuberant burst of energy at the starter's gun. Pick specific moments in the race: the feeling of power as you surge uphill, the release and joy of flying downhill, and finally the sense of triumph as you reach the finish line in thirty-eight minutes or less.

Or, if you wish, you might focus your awareness on the cellular level, imaging your red blood cells absorbing oxygen more efficiently than usual. Combine this visualization with several deep breaths, giving your red cells a chance to practice in the material realm what you are experiencing in the mental realm.

*To increase your creativity.*   Start with the assumption that creativity is a natural human state and that, potentially, your ability to create, to put together the stuff of existence in novel ways, is limitless. Place your left hand, palm down, on your *hara*. Place your right hand on your upper chest. Breathe so that your left hand rises and falls with each breath while the right hand remains motionless. Once you've established this deep belly breathing, place your hands on the floor, palms up, a few inches out from your sides. Allow the breath to enter through your nostrils and travel downward as if to fill the abdomen. Exhale consciously through the mouth until your lungs are as empty as is comfortably possible. At this point of emptiness, as in Focused Surrender (chapter 5), simply close your mouth. The incoming breath arises spontaneously. The precise moment of its coming is unexpected, a delightful little surprise. When the incoming breath has again traveled downward as if to fill the belly, open your mouth and exhale consciously. Repeat the cycle several times.

This simple breathing technique shows the subtle, crucial relationship between what is willed and what is spontaneous, between the conscious and the subconscious. Magda Proskauer, a master of breathing techniques, has called the brief interval between outgoing and incoming breath the "creative pause." During this moment of pure, unwilled being, you can experience the impulse of creation that arises, unbidden, from the depths of each of us.

Continue this mode of breathing. Now, elbows out to the sides, touch your forehead gently with the tips of your fingers while you are consciously exhaling. When the incoming breath spontaneously comes in through your nostrils, let your arms open wide in synchrony with the incoming breath. It is as if you are breathing in the whole universe. During your conscious exhalation, bring your arms together, until your fingertips gently touch your throat. Again open your arms in synchrony with the incoming breath. Repeat this cycle, touching your heart, solar plexis, *hara*, and pubis in turn, thus invoking bodily centers that are sometimes associated with thought, expressiveness, feeling, power, intuitive action, and generation.

Now lie in the relaxation position, hands palm up by your sides, and bring to mind some creative project. See and feel yourself operating with effortless, joyful creativity. Experience the delight of making new connections, of gaining insights that seem to come from the creative void, from "nowhere." Experience the fun of creative work with others. Consider the creative possibilities in every life, not just in art and "creative writing" and the like but in management, in love and sex, in gardening, entertaining, and household chores. Think of the creativity latent in every moment of time.

Finish this exercise, as with every imaging exercise, in an attitude of acceptance, thanksgiving, and alignment with God or the universe.

We offer these samples simply to trigger your creativity. We believe that you can find a uniquely personal imaging procedure for any transformation of your body and psyche you sincerely desire. Our experience has shown us that such procedures are highly effective in most cases.

It's possible that you'll experience quick changes for the better but don't expect immediate results. Learning and change tend to take place in irregular spurts of progress separated by long periods on the plateau, with no apparent gain. But the plateau represents the esssential topography of all human development. Even quick changes must be followed by diligent practice if they are to be permanent. Keep practicing diligently and you can be reasonably sure the gains will eventually come.

The ITP Kata concludes in the next chapter.

# EIGHT

# The ITP Kata: Meditation

We now move to the Kata's last exercise, a ten-minute period of meditation. By "meditation" we mean the disciplined observation of thoughts, feelings, impulses, and sensations, as well as the spontaneous turning of heart and mind toward a Presence beyond the ordinary self. This practice, which combines self-observation with what is sometimes called "contemplative prayer," helps practitioners contact new depths of being, awareness, and delight.

The American philosopher William James described the transformative power of meditation and prayer. The further limits of human nature, he wrote,

> plunge into an altogether other dimension of existence from the sensible and merely "understandable" world. Name it the mystical region, or the supernatural region, whichever you choose. So far as our ideal impulses originate in this region (and most of them do originate in it, for we find them possessing us in a way for which we cannot articulately account), we belong to it in a more intimate sense than that in which we belong to the visible world, for we belong in the most intimate sense wherever our ideals belong. Yet the unseen region in question is not merely ideal, for it produces effects in this world. When we commune with it, work is actually done upon our finite personality, for we are turned into new men, and consequences in the way of conduct follow in the natural world upon our regenerative change.

**A New Buoyancy and Sense of Freedom**

In the ITP Kata, meditation begins as soon as you have finished imaging and induction. Assume a sitting position with back straight, on a floor cushion with your legs crossed, or in a chair. An erect sitting posture, either on a cushion that elevates your seat from the ground or in a straight-backed chair, will help you remain alert for the exercise to follow. It will also help prevent the muscular soreness that poor posture causes. If during the exercise you find yourself slumping, straighten your spine and rebalance yourself. During meditation, a good physical attitude facilitates a good psychological attitude. An alert but relaxed posture tends to produce an alertly poised state of mind. In this, the body and the inner life mirror one another.

Place your attention a few feet in front of you. Do not stare or strain to concentrate. Instead, maintain a relaxed focus, as if you were gazing at a gentle stream. This style of attention, this soft downward look, is not as fatiguing as staring. It also helps to keep your mind from drifting. You can, however, meditate with eyes closed, but if you do, you might have a tendency to drift into sleep. Meditation with eyes open will help you stay relaxed but alert.

When your posture is comfortable, let your belly expand. Make sure that your breath is not confined to your chest. Full, relaxed respiration, in which both the lower and upper abdomen are involved, is more conductive to meditation than constricted breathing, which typically causes or is caused by anxiety. Anchor your attention in the rise and fall of your breath. Focus on your lower abdomen and return to it whenever your mind wanders.

As your posture, gaze, and respiration join to form a state of alert relaxation, remain calmly present to your stream of consciousness, to both its familiar and unfamiliar patterns. Do not judge yourself, for in meditation of this kind there is no "good" or "bad." At this stage of practice, you are simply deepening your self-awareness, whatever it brings to light. You are getting more intimate with yourself. You are gently exercising new control of your mind and exploring new depths of your body and soul. Here are some questions meditation beginners typically ask.

*What do you do if you can't escape a repetitive thought or particular mood?* If an object of awareness won't pass, simply study it and let it unfold. If it is a relatively familiar set of thoughts or feelings, you can note new subtleties and nuances in it. No two moods or mental pictures are exactly the same, even when they seem to be. Your inner life is endlessly mutable, and your most familiar patterns of consciousness nearly always contain something new. Wait for that newness to reveal itself. It might show you something important. One of our students, for example, was obsessed by a childhood fall from a tree. In meditation, she found herself focusing—again and again—on the smell and feel, the shock, and the pain of her accident, which had happened some twenty years before. For several weeks in which the memory dominated her meditation, she witnessed more and more details of the tree, of her sweater and jeans, of her emotions as she looked at the leaves around her, of her grip on the slippery branches. Then, suddenly, she experienced it all in a new way, from another vantage point. Now she looked down on her fall, as if she were the sky itself. All at once, her fright was gone. The fall even had the feel of flight. From then on, the memory didn't haunt her meditation. More importantly, she felt a new liberation in the rest of her life. Her consciousness had expanded, it seems, so that it could embrace her memories of the accident—and life in general—with new security.

Disciplined self-observation can yield results analogous to those of our student. If you remain calmly present to a persistent image or mood, you might see an old trauma in a new light, discover new qualities in a familiar situation, or find new solutions to a pressing problem.

***Does the relinquishment of thoughts interfere with creative thinking? Don't we risk losing a bright idea if we let it go?*** No. Experience teaches us that creative insights persist. As writers, we have learned that good ideas come back when formal meditation is done. If an idea is worth remembering, you will remember it.

***What do you do about physical discomfort?*** Straighten your back, rebalance yourself, and relax. If the discomfort persists, sit through it. One of meditation's great lessons is that pain can be released through calm awareness of it. There is a profound analogy here to those problems in life that are dealt with best by embracing them without avoidance.

***What do you do with your hands?*** They can be placed on your knees, as they are in many Indian yogas, or cupped in your lap with your thumbs touching, as they are in most Zen practice. Either way is fine. Experiment, then stick with one method so that you can deepen your concentration without physical distraction.

*Why does one need to sit still?* Because physical stillness facilitates mental stillness, and the complex set of physiological changes called the "relaxation response" (see p. 114). Eventually, the centered poise produced by sitting meditation can be taken into every activity of everyday life. Meditation in action is a primary goal of integral practice.

*Can one repeat a word, a mantra, to help focus attention?* Yes. Mental repetition of a phrase has long been used in meditation as a concentration device. You can experiment with a word or short sentence to see if it helps focus your mind. But to repeat: Once you have settled on a concentration method that works, whether it is focusing on your breath, a mantra, or your stream of consciousness, stick with it. Moving from one technique to another can distract you from the deeper rewards of meditation.

*Sometimes meditation gives rise to strange experiences. How should they be dealt with?* Many an unusual experience is reported by meditators, among them distortions of body image, perceptions of "auras," sensations of rising from the ground, and auditions of sounds with no apparent physical causes. Remain calmly present to such experiences, as if they are ordinary thoughts and feelings. By staying centered, you will let them reveal whatever lessons they can teach. They are a natural by-product of sustained meditation practice and might be first glimpses of metanormal abilities. If they persist, there are two ways to handle them: first, simply let them go until they subside entirely; and second, let them unfold to reveal a latent capacity. Using the second approach, one of our students cultivated the perception of auras that her meditation triggered. Such perceptions were uncomfortable at first, but eventually became a source of information and pleasure.

*How do we know if we are becoming enlightened?* We do not use the term "enlightenment" in our ITP programs, partly because it is used in different and sometimes confusing ways, and partly because we emphasize practice itself rather than specific outcomes. If by "enlightenment" you simply mean the greater goods of meditation, those will come by degrees, often unexpectedly, especially if you do not compulsively strive for them.

***Some books about personal growth talk about a higher, truer, or deeper being beyond one's ordinary sense of self. Does meditation help us discover it?*** Meditation deepens an awareness that transcends your ordinary functioning. As you continue meditating, you realize that you are more than any idea or mental picture, more than any emotion, more than any impulse, more than any bodily process, more than any pattern of experience with which you typically identify. That something more, you will find, brings an unshakable security, freedom, and delight. You might experience it as a boundless space, or unbroken essence, that connects you with everything. From it, you can realize new mastery of mind and body.

This depth beyond ordinary feeling and thought is given different names by sages and philosophers and is characterized in different ways in the various sacred traditions. But however it is described and no matter how it blossoms, it produces a new buoyancy and unity with the world at large.

The deeper being that meditation brings is its own reward. It is also helpful—and we believe necessary—for the practical success of integral discipline. That is the case because its regenerative freedom helps cushion the readjustments and restructurings of body and mind required for significant change. Its all-encompassing embrace helps sustain a radical renewal of our entire organism. Because it transcends our particular parts, it helps us rise above the many obstacles to growth we encounter.

## "A Special Draft Upon the Unseen"

In the course of meditation, many people experience a gratitude for life that impels them to commune with a higher power. In contemplative traditions that do not bear witness to a personal divinity, the devotional urge is expressed in prayerful chanting, either silent or vocal, as in Zen Buddhism and Indian Vedanta. The sense of blessedness that deep meditation bestows turns the heart toward the source of things. Meditation naturally turns to that source, asking for nothing more than loving contact with it.

Frederic Myers, a principal founder of modern psychical research and pioneering personality theorist, believed that in prayer we intensify a process that is always happening in us. He wrote in *Human Personality and Its Survival of Bodily Death:*

I have spoken of it as a fluctuation in the intensity of the draft which each man's life makes upon the Unseen. I have urged that while our life is maintained by continual inflow from the World-Soul, that inflow may vary in abundance or energy in correspondence with variations in the attitude of our minds. . . . The supplication of the Lourdes pilgrims, the adoring contemplation of the Christian Scientists, the inward concentration of the self-suggesters, the trustful anticipation of the hypnotized subject—all these are mere shades of the same mood of mind—of the mountain-moving faith which can in actual fact draw fresh life from the Infinite.

Each of us can draw upon the Unseen for transformations beyond the purview of mainstream science. Some members of our classes, for example, have experienced remissions from afflictions that many doctors think are incurable. But although science cannot explain such remissions (and other kinds of extraordinary experience described in this book), there is a growing body of research that supports anecdotal reports of such changes produced by transformative practices. By 2003, for example, more than 2,000 studies published in reputable journals had shown that meditation can have many desirable outcomes. In their monograph, *The Physical and Psychological Effects of Meditation*, Michael Murphy, Steven Donovan, and Margaret Livingston published a review of such studies, which have shown that meditation can help to:

lower resting heart rate;

reduce both systolic and diastolic blood pressure (including systolic reductions of 25 mm Hg or more);

produce significant changes in cortical activity, among them increased frequency and amplitude of alpha waves (8–12 cycles per second), strong bursts of theta waves (4–8 cycles per second), and the synchronization of alpha waves between brain hemispheres, all of which indicate that meditators experience a state of alert relaxation and perhaps increased brain efficiency;

increase respiratory efficiency while the meditator is sitting and also while engaged in strenuous activity;

reduce muscle tension;

reduce blood lactate concentrations associated with anxiety and high blood pressure;

increase skin resistance, which indicates a lowering of anxiety and stress;

increase salivary translucence, while decreasing salivary proteins and bacteria, all of which helps to prevent tooth cavities;

reduce chronic pain;

heighten visual sensitivity, auditory acuity, and the discrimination of musical tones;

improve reaction time and responsive motor skills;

improve the ability to make visual and kinesthetic discriminations in spite of misleading stimuli from the environment (an ability that is correlated with independence of judgment and a strong sense of body and self);

improve concentration;

increase empathy for other people;

reduce anxiety;

help relieve addictions;

improve memory and general intelligence;

increase equanimity;

promote feelings of pleasure and ecstasy;

increase energy and healthy excitement; and

increase dream recall.

These benefits come without the meditator striving for them. They are among the graces of transformative practice. But along with these, meditation can have negative outcomes for certain people. Some psychologists have reported, for example, that it can intensify obsessiveness, divert attention from genuine problems, and contribute to feelings of depression. That is why we have insisted that members of our ITP classes take care of their emotional needs in appropriate ways, seeking counsel when needed.

That meditation can have negative, as well as positive, results has long been noted in the contemplative literature. The way to spiritual liberation is "sharp as the razor's edge," reads the Katha Upanishad, one of India's most revered scriptures. Though the rewards of meditation can be great, they do not come without disciplined self-knowledge. That is why we have placed meditation within the context of integral practice, which emphasizes the long-term development of health, self-awareness, and balance.

## A Great Return on Your Investment

Practiced properly, meditation is a richly efficient means of self-transformation. Like a good business deal or scientific theory, it produces great returns on investment of time and energy. Economically, it enhances many of our inborn capacities. In this respect, it resembles imagery practice and other transformative modalities that draw upon various human endowments to produce several fruitful results at once.

Herbert Benson, a physician who has pioneered research on the relations of mind and body, invented the term "relaxation response" to represent the integrated changes produced by contemplative activity. With other researchers, he has emphasized the fact that meditation produces multiple benefits by activating the parasympathetic nervous system, which mediates the slowing of heart rate and respiration, reduction of muscle tension, and other components of relaxation. Meditation *economically* produces many good results because it triggers a coordinated response of our whole organism. We emphasize this observation because it applies as well to other integrated changes produced by transformative practices. Creative work and athletic discipline, for example, facilitate a condition that resembles certain inherited behaviors of animals in the wild. Like hunting (or hunted) animals, many artists and athletes exhibit a trancelike focus of attention, an indifference to discomfort and pain, and a remarkable forgetting of difficulty. The deep concentration, analgesia, and selective amnesia that characterize creative absorption is analogous to—and may be derived from—the freezing and stalking behaviors, freedom from pain, and blindness to adversity that is evident among hunting animals. Like the relaxation response, creative absorption economically enlists many psychosomatic processes.

And a similar enlistment of inborn tendencies is evident in sports and the martial arts when a contest stimulates heart rate, adrenaline flow, and strong bursts of energy. The fight-or-flight response, like the relaxation response and creative absorption, is part of our common human endowment, and can be enlisted for transformative activity. It, too, operates synergistically and can facilitate the development of mind and flesh.

In *The Future of the Body*, Michael Murphy suggests that all transformative modalities have some of this "all-at-once" character, by which they produce creative change in a coordinated manner. Imagery practice can give rise to metanormal powers and consciousness by the recruitment of many somatic processes. Through such recruitment, countless cells are somehow enlisted by mental images so that *as an integrated whole* they support extraordinary functioning. Similarly, the repetition of affirmations, sustained expectation of success, focused intention, surrender to ego-transcending powers, and other transformative acts can trigger complex changes in us. All programs for healing and growth depend upon such responses, and integral practice is no exception. Drawing upon the wisdom inherent in religious and other transformative disciplines, we have incorporated activities with an "all-at-once" character into the program described in this book.

## Lasting Benefits

Our Kata ends with meditation, but in a fundamental sense it is not finished then. Several years of ITP classes have taught us that this set of exercises often produces an afterglow. Typically, its results spill into one's everyday activities. The ongoing effects of repeated affirmations, the pleasure of exercised muscles and ligaments, the multiple benefits of imagery and meditation last longer than the Kata itself. That is the ultimate reward of this forty-minute practice.

The Taoist saying "meditation in action is a hundred, a thousand, a million times greater than meditation in repose" reflects the aim of integral discipline. The exercises described here are meant to join meditation with action in every part of our lives. New freshness of perception, increased empathy for others, alert relaxation, enhanced sensory-motor skills, and other improvements of mind and body have been evident in members of our classes, as they have been in the contemplative traditions and scientific studies of meditation.

NINE

# *The Exercise Factor*

The strong relationship between regular physical exercise and good health has been established beyond all doubt. Reports of scientific studies on what exercise can do for you appear frequently in the popular press. The benefits are many and varied, and we'll list them later in this chapter. In Integral Transformative Practice, however, we prefer to view vigorous physical movement not as a mechanical process that yields so many benefits for so much effort expended, but rather as a fundamental expression of our embodiment, essential to our practice precisely because it is valuable *for its own sake*. In ITP, we repeat this phrase, "for its own sake," like a prayer or incantation.

In this culture, as we have pointed out, we are relentlessly urged to do one thing only for the sake of something else—some goal, some reward, something not here, not now: something in the future. Early in life, we are urged to study hard so that we'll get good grades. We're told to get good grades so that we'll graduate from high school and get into college, so that we'll get a good job. We're told to get a good job so that we can buy a house and a car. We spend our lives stretched on an iron rack of contingencies. Clearly, contingencies are important. Goals are important. But the real juice of life is to be found not nearly so much in the products of our efforts as in the process of living itself, in how it feels to be alive.

We were born, it seems to us, with a God-given right to move vigorously, gracefully, and joyfully. Our being so often robbed of this right constitutes a major tragedy of our civilization, one that can be traced in large part to the denigration of the body common to most civilized societies as well as to the mind-body split that has dominated Western thought for some three hundred years. In this milieu, the body has been considered an object, an instrument, a brute machine of gratification and procreation. At the height of the Victorian period, in fact, members of polite society often seemed to vacate the body entirely, making it a topic to be rarely considered or mentioned. Now we are beginning to reinhabit our bodies, beginning to see this most extraordinary of entities for what it is.

Far from being a mere machine, the human body is the most advanced material realization we've encountered of the divine potential hidden in the early, inchoate universe. Each body is all time remembered. In its dancing quanta of radiation, its elementary particles, its atoms and ions, its simple and complex molecules, its cells and organelles and organs, its bone and marrow and muscle and sinew, we can read the story of cosmic evolution, that chronicle of exquisite joinings and hairbreadth escapes, which has created a consciousness capable of knowing itself.

To live is to move. Even when seemingly motionless in sleep, the body is incessantly moving. We share a silent pulsing of heart, blood vessels, glands, diaphragm, lungs—the busy intercourse among a hundred trillion cells—with many other organisms. When we consciously move through space, we can't help but affirm what is both unique and universal about our species.

## Our Commitment to Exercise

We ask that everyone involved in Integral Transformative Practice accomplish a minimum of three hours of aerobic exercise every week in increments of at least twenty minutes each. The word *aerobic* means "using air to live." During aerobic exercise, the rate at which oxygen reaches the muscles keeps pace with the rate at which it is used. Thus, the muscles operate without having to dip into their reserves of sugar and fat, as is the case with *anaerobic* exercise. In aerobic exercise, you are breathing more deeply and rapidly than while at rest but can still carry on a conversation.

This aerobic exercise commitment can be fulfilled simply by taking vigorous twenty-minute walks nine times a week. For greater benefits, we highly recommend three sessions of strength training a week. Whatever exercise you do, we urge you to exercise with full awareness. Don't read, watch television, or daydream. Our experience shows that by keeping your mind focused on what you are doing, you can greatly increase the intrinsic pleasure of vigorous movement, as well as the benefits you receive.

### To Walk, to Run, To Be Human

Walking is one of the most commonplace of human activities. It is also a great wonder—stately, graceful, and efficient, an essential mark of being human. The journey of our lineage toward the large brain, culture and consciousness took a decisive and irreversible turn with the evolutionary gamble of the upright stance and unique bipedal walking of our hominid ancestors. We are so accustomed to it that we are unaware of how marvelous walking is. To see this form of movement as if for the first time, use a lens that turns things upside down or (if you're willing to look a little foolish) lean over so that your head is upside down. From this perspective, a group of people walking toward you reveals an amazingly supple, undulating movement, an easy, liquid flow of energy unlike that of any other creature.

To take three brisk hour-long or six thirty-minute or nine twenty-minute walks every week would fulfill your ITP aerobic exercise commitment, yield proven health benefits, and help build the foundation for possible transformations—and do all this with a minimal risk of injury. Does this mean you should walk merely to gain benefits, to fulfill your commitment? Better, we think, that you walk primarily for the joy of it. Walk to experience the upright stance, the flow of motion through space and time. Walk with full awareness of your legs and arms swinging freely in perfect counterpoise. Walk with a spring in your steps. Walk with shoulders, neck, chest, and abdomen relaxed. Be aware of the back as well as the front of your body. Give special attention to your physical center, a point an inch or so beneath the navel. Imagine your center moving powerfully and effortlessly through space. Take deep breaths. *Be sure to walk vigorously*. A casual stroll doesn't qualify as aerobic exercise.

*Walking downhill, quickly become weightless. Walking uphill, slowly become your strength.*

M.M.

Whenever possible, walk out of doors rather than on an indoor treadmill, satisfying the innate human desire to explore the world, to discover new vistas. Seek out hills to climb. Wear a loaded backpack to develop added leg strength—or to carry supplies for a picnic. Don't be limited to the minimum ITP commitment. Take extended hikes, gradually increasing the distance. Walk instead of using your car whenever possible. It's possible, but difficult, to walk too much.

Running ups the ante, adding possibilities and risks. When we walk, one foot is always earthbound, but when we run, we leave the ground. The earth becomes our drum, and the rhythm of our drumming feet presages the quickened pulse of heart and blood. The face flushes, and we feel the rush of air on cheeks and forehead. Breathing deepens. We experience the beginnings of a familiar exultation along with a touch of fear, a momentary catch in the breath. It is a feeling of vertiginous anticipation and delicious dread akin to the first awareness of sexual arousal. Running, we can no longer deny our animal nature. At the same time, we are uniquely human, for no other animal runs as we do.

Running in our singular upright stance confronts us with a seeming contradiction: the human runner is relatively slow and the energy cost of running (oxygen consumption per unit of body weight per unit of distance) is about twice as high for humans as for most other mammals. Yet, in a long chase, a well-conditioned runner can catch a horse, deer, wildebeest, zebra, kangaroo, or pronghorn antelope. This is due not only to the intelligence and fierce determination of our species but also to our unsurpassed ability to dissipate heat, along with the ability to load up on carbohydrates and the virtuosity of our breathing. To run long distances, especially with a partner or a group, is to summon our primal past: the profusion of healthy sweat, the lusty breaths, the glory of distance traveled, the shouts of triumph as the prey is overtaken. Some people these days call running a fad or even an addiction, a form of narcissism. But to call running a fad makes as much sense as to call thinking a fad. Endurance running is an essential human activity that preceded abstract thought and helped make it possible.

Still, there are risks. The chances of falling or of spraining an ankle or twisting a knee increase as we shift from a walk to a run. Even more prevalent and troublesome are the persistent, often tricky overuse injuries that can bring debilitating pain and dysfunction to cartilage, tendon, ligament, and joint. Overuse is compounded by the long-term repetitive motion that runners often fall into—the same stride, the same joint movement, the same pounding impact. There's a dangerously hypnotic quality that accompanies running long distances at a steady pace and stride. To avoid overuse and repetitive motion injury, we recommend awareness, variety, and playfulness.

Shine an interior spotlight of awareness on parts of your physique that are subject to undue strain. See if you can relieve that strain by making subtle adjustments in the way you're moving. In some cases, just relaxing the arms can release the rigidity of your stride and increase its grace and efficiency. Check for tension everywhere in the body. There are few sights more dismaying than that of runners with high shoulders and rigid necks and jaws, stamping all this tension into body and psyche with every stride. The secret of power, whatever your sport, lies in relaxation. Every muscle except those being used specifically for locomotion at any given moment should be quite relaxed. Whether running primarily for health and fitness, speed, endurance, or transformation, the runner's first discipline involves releasing tightness, especially of the face, neck, shoulders, chest, and diaphram.

It's also important not to get locked into an unvarying, mechanical motion. Change the length and bounce of your stride. Alternate longer-than-usual with shorter-than-usual strides. Or take an especially long stride, a leap, every third step. Or try skipping. (Don't laugh. Skipping may be better than jogging for aerobic conditioning, while leading to fewer injuries.) If you should find yourself running on a smooth, straight, unobstructed path, try running backward, an essential practice for defensive backs in football. Or try running sideways, crossing the feet alternately, scissors style.

Vary your speed. It was once thought that aerobics meant attaining a certain target heart rate and holding it steady for thirty minutes or more. In recent years, however, researchers have found that varying your heart rate doesn't rob you of aerobic benefits. As it turns out, periodic as well as continuous exercise holds great value; it's all right to stop for a while during a run—or a walk—and stretch for relaxation or just enjoy the view.

Don't confine yourself to the same route on every run. Venture into new territory. Take routes you've never tried before, especially those that lead up and down hills. Work out a steeplechase, a sort of runner's obstacle course, with ditches to leap, walls to run on or jump over, trees and bushes to dodge. But start cautiously. After years of running steadily on smooth, predictable surfaces, you'll need time to reawaken your coordination.

Above all, use your imagination. If you're training for a competitive run, you're pretty well committed to an essentially linear activity. But there's also nonlinear running. With a Frisbee, a friend, and an open field, for example, you can easily devise a sport that will yield twenty or more delightful minutes of aerobics. Start twenty or thirty paces apart and launch the Frisbee in your friend's general direction, then start running at a comfortable pace in such a way as to maintain about the same distance between the two of you. Keep moving as the Frisbee sails back and forth, varying your pace as necessary to catch the flying disk. Similar sports can be devised using anything from a tennis ball to a football. The parabolic curve of a ball in flight adds another element to your running. By catching it, you make visible your intuitive knowledge of the laws of physics. Many ball sports that involve running—tennis, volleyball, racquetball, squash, basketball—can also be made aerobic by switching from a competitive to a collaborative mode, the idea being to keep the ball in play as much as possible and to run at a moderate rate most of the time.

No matter how moderate, though, there's still that lingering chance of overuse and repetitive motion injuries for those who run long distances. To minimize the risk, choose good-fitting, high-quality running shoes and replace them often. (Running shoes lose their tread and their resilience much more quickly than do auto tires.) Run on natural surfaces, on the good earth itself, as much as possible, or on composition tracks. If you must run on city streets, look for asphalt surfaces. Keep your body flexible, but bear in mind that it's not necessary to stretch just before running. In fact, it's not a good idea to stretch while the muscles are cold and subject to injury. Better to start with a few minutes warm-up along with the articulation of the body's joints—just what you get in the ITP Kata. Stretching *after* a run is better than stretching cold.

After all of this has been said, there's still one big constraint: Those of us with heavy body builds might consider taking up something other than running as our main long-term mode of aerobic exercise. Even easy jogging sends a heavy impact to the joints. Your feet, ankles, and knees take a jolt of several times your body weight with each stride. Almost everyone can enjoy the exhilaration of running, but a light or medium body build is generally prerequisite to choosing running as your main, long-term mode of aerobic conditioning. And bear in mind that brisk walking offers most of the health benefits of running with few of the risks.

*Practice mentally for physical activities. Practice physically for mental activities.*

G.L.

### The Varieties of Aerobic Experience

If we have given what seems a disproportionate amount of space to aerobic running, it's simply because that primal activity presents us with a disproportionate number of both risks and possibilities and thus demands discussion. There are many other ways of fulfilling your weekly aerobic commitment.

Swimming is an ideal conditioning sport, especially for people of medium and heavy build. It works all of your body. It doesn't subject your shins and joints to the pounding of the running sports. In the weightless, sensuous environment of water, in fact, you have your very best chance of getting fit without getting hurt. The down side of this virtual weightlessness is that, in not stressing the bones, swimming doesn't build bone tissue as the the weight-bearing sports do. Then too, there are the problems of finding a conveniently located pool and overcoming the boredom of swimming laps, the latter of which can be remedied by creating aerobic water games. Even better, you might learn to love the cool, wet, solitary world of the swimmer, even when cruising back and forth from one end of a pool to the other.

Gliding across the earth on a bicycle at the pleasant speed of 12 to 15 mph on softly spinning wheels as both passenger and motor, you can get aerobics along with a sense of freedom. Not only can you travel much farther than a runner in a given period, you can do so without the pounding motion that stresses sinews and joints. The worst biking injuries come from falling off or, worst yet, being struck by another, larger vehicle. Wear your helmet! Pain in the neck and shoulders, lower back, wrists, knees, and feet—to name a few sites— generally are caused by improper alignment with the machine. Check with an expert or a knowledgeable friend to adjust seat and handlebar height and angle.

Then you have rowing, cross-country skiing, skating, skateblading, and the fruit of whatever fitness technology comes next.

Given sufficient imagination and will, aerobic activities are there for the finding. You can jump rope, bounce on a trampoline, shadow box. You can take aerobic classes. You can dance aerobically and thus participate in one of the most primal of activities: There are cultures with no permanent dwelling places, no tool or weapon other than the stick and stone, no clothing other than the loin cloth, no plastic art, but there are no human cultures without music and dance. You can create martial arts routines that are aerobic in nature. And if it's in your nature, you can make an even more primal activity, sexual intercourse, the basis of an aerobic workout. Any happily vigorous activity that uses several muscle groups, especially those long muscles that attach to the pelvic girdle, will grant you the gift of sweat and lusty breathing.

If all else fails, you have the aerobic machines that allow you to keep moving while not getting anywhere. Actually, there's a certain value in treadmills, stationary bicycles, and step machines, in that they allow you precise control of your workouts with a minimal risk of injury. In Integral Transformative Practice, however, we ask that even when using stationary indoor machines you exercise with full awareness rather than reading or watching television. Our experience has clearly shown that energy follows attention, that staying aware of your breath, the articulation of your joints, and the contraction and relaxation of sinew and muscle can significantly improve the quality of your exercise. Most of all, we ask that you do your aerobic exercise primarily for the joy of it. The benefits will come. Here's a list of some of them:

Healthily enlarged and strengthened heart muscle

Increased cardiac output

Lower resting heart rate

Increased hemoglobin levels

Increased venous return

Increased maximum oxygen uptake

Improved circulation

Decreased blood pressure

Greater bone mass

Decreased degeneration of joints and ligaments

Increased muscular strength

Improved reaction time

Increased ability to utilize fats and carbohydrates

Decreased body fat

Increased "good cholesterol" (HDL); less "bad cholesterol" (LDL)

Improved mobilization of lactic acid

Improved hormonal balance

Increased blood clot–dissolving enzymes

Strengthened immune system

Reduction in coronary heart disease

Improved resistance to cancer

Improved mental functioning and psychological health

In our own experimental work, as noted earlier, the 12.60 percent average reduction in body fat among our 1993 ITP class correlated strongly with the time students spent doing aerobic exercise. Still, with all this, there are negative possibilities. Exercise can produce or contribute to overcompetitiveness, excessive fatigue from overtraining, preoccupation with diet, obsession with body image, neglect of job or family, general self-centeredness, and physical injuries. As in any form of self-cultivation, physical training calls for intelligence, balance, and good judgment in order to produce good results.

## MUSCLES VS. AGING

Our strong recommendation that you add three sessions of strength training to your weekly exercise schedule gains urgency from research showing the close relationship between muscle mass and strength on the one hand and quality of life on the other, especially as it concerns aging. The practice of ITP, as we've stated earlier, should be available to as many people as possible, regardless of physical or financial status. We also believe that there should be no upper-age limit; aging is a process that involves every one of us. And, as it turns out, muscle strength and mass are crucially important factors as we travel toward the culmination of the life we are given. In their book, *Biomarkers*, William J. Evans, Ph.D., and Irwin H. Rosenberg, M.D., list ten "biomarkers" of aging and show how all ten can be favorably altered, thus alleviating much of the debility that accompanies old age. They are:

1. Your Muscle Mass

2. Your Strength

3. Your Basal Metabolic Rate (BMR)

4. Your Body Fat Percentage

5. Your Aerobic Capacity

6. Your Body's Blood-Sugar Tolerance

7. Your Cholesterol/HDL Ratio

8. Your Blood Pressure

9. Your Bone Density

10. Your Body's Ability to Regulate Its Internal Temperature

Of these ten, according to Evans and Rosenberg, muscle mass and strength are primary. They write that a high ratio of muscle to fat in the body

> causes the metabolism to rise, meaning you can more easily burn body fat and alter your body composition even further in favor of beneficial muscle tissue;

> increases your aerobic capacity—and the health of your whole cardiovascular system—because you have more working muscles consuming oxygen;

> triggers muscle to use more insulin, thus greatly reducing the chances you'll ever develop diabetes;

helps maintain higher levels of the beneficial HDL cholesterol in your blood.

But can this simple prescription—bigger and stronger muscles—really alter the aging picture, as Evans and Rosenberg claim? We're all familiar with the studies on aging, the books, the articles, all showing the seemingly inevitable, irreversible decline in abilities that comes with the passing years. Aerobic ability, for example, seems to fall off at a rate of some 8 to 10 percent for every ten years after age twenty. On average, we lose almost seven pounds of muscle every decade. From age twenty to around age seventy, we lose nearly 30 percent of our muscle cells. Our basal metabolic rate—the ability to transform food into energy and build tissue—declines by an estimated 2 percent a decade starting at age twenty. And so it goes, a dismal picture of degeneration and decay.

We're not going to say that the studies are wrong per se. But they are terribly misleading. What they measure in most cases is a cross section of our population *as it is now*—that is to say, a population that becomes increasingly sedentary as it ages. Even the longitudinal studies, those that follow the same group of people over a number of years, fail by and large to consider the exercise regimen of the people they follow.

"Most of the decline in physical functioning is caused not by aging but by lack of exercise," says William Evans. "Once we leave school, most of us spend less time exercising, for obvious reasons—family, job, lack of opportunity. Or we think we *shouldn't* exercise *because* we're getting older. So what we have is a self-fulfilling prophecy; we get weak and frail and assume it's because we're getting old. This just isn't true. We compared young men who underwent endurance training with men between forty-five and sixty years old who had the same training and found that aerobic capacity and percentage of body fat is related to the time spent exercising—not to age. In this study, age did not predict anything."

How about muscular strength and size? It's an old truism in physical conditioning that strength falls off rapidly with the years and that even if the muscles of the elderly can be made a bit stronger, they can't be made larger.

Wrong again. Walter Frontera, M.D., Ph.D., then at the Human Nutrition Research Center on Aging at Tufts University at Boston, put twelve men between the ages of sixty and seventy-two through a course of rather intense weight lifting, three days a week for twelve weeks, concentrating on the quadriceps and hamstrings (the front and back thigh muscles). The result surprised even the most optimistic exercise enthusiasts. The strength of the men's quadriceps more than doubled and that of the hamstrings tripled, with an average *daily* gain of 3.3 percent and 6.5 percent respectively. The real shocker was that the men's muscles had grown an average of 12 percent.

What about even older people? Also at Tufts, Maria A. Fiatarone, M.D., put ten men and women between eighty-seven and ninety-six years of age, living in a chronic-care hospital, through a similar training regimen. After only *eight* weeks, their leg muscle strength almost tripled and their thigh muscles bulked up by more than 10 percent. The researchers concluded that, contrary to all conventional wisdom on the subject, *muscle growth in people ranging from sixty to ninety-six years old was as great as could be expected in young people doing the same amount of exercise.*

Integral Transformative Practice is not an antiaging program. It is a practice for achieving the transformative potential of all people, whatever their age, gender, or background. Still, we feel this evidence of adaptability and resilience in the very old can serve as an inspiration to us all, an invitation to live fully and physically, whatever our age. The evidence shows that it's neither necessary nor wise to let your muscles wither away with the passing of the years.

## BUILDING AND MAINTAINING MUSCLES

Muscle strength and size is maintained or increased by working the muscles against strong resistance. This is most often accomplished by using Nautilus-type machines, lifting free weights, or working against the weight of your own body. Joining a gym or health club is ideal. Machines are generally safer as well as more muscle-specific and conducive to good form than are free weights, especially for beginners. Guidance from experienced trainers, always important, should be available at the beginning of your participation and at regular intervals thereafter. *Again, exercise with full awareness.* This is especially important in strength training. In Arnold Schwarzenegger's words, "A pump when I picture the muscle I want is worth ten with my mind drifting."

With free weights, it's even more important that you have some hands-on guidance at the start. Neither books nor videotapes, no matter how well done, can give you the kind of feedback about form that will get you the best results and help you avoid injury. Books and tapes, though, do become quite useful *after* some personal guidance. With your own free weights, you can work out at home, avoiding the cost and inconvenience of going to a gym.

What if you have neither free weights or access to a gym? You still don't have to let your muscles languish. Note that the ITP Kata offers a certain amount of strength training (see chapter 6). The Fountain requires the half squat, one of the best ways of working the muscles of the legs and buttocks. For strength training, try doing not just the six that are required for the Kata but ten or twenty— however many you're capable of. Then rest for one to two minutes and repeat. Same thing with the curl-ups, which strengthen the all-important abdominal muscles. The Sun Salutation exercises several muscle groups, notably the lower back muscles. The quad tightening offers isometric exercise for the quadriceps. By adding just three more of these self-loaded exercises, you can maintain or increase the strength and size of the most essential muscle groups:

*The athlete that dwells in each of us is more than an abstract ideal. It is a living presence that can change the way we feel and live.*

G.L.

***Push-ups.*** With your hands and toes on the floor and arms and legs straight, lower your chest to the floor, bending the elbows, keeping the body straight. Then push up from the floor and back to the starting position. If this is too hard, leave your knees on the floor when pushing up. If even this is too hard, start with wall push-ups, leaning toward a wall with arms extended, then bending and extending the arms. If the standard push-up is too easy, elevate the legs by placing your feet on a sturdy stool or chair. Move slowly and smoothly up and down, and keep going until you can no longer rise from the floor. Rest for one to two minutes, then repeat the exercise.

***Dips.*** Place two sturdy chairs (that won't move when you do this exercise) far enough apart so that you can sit on the edge of one and place your feet on the edge of the other. Put your hands, palms down with arms straight, on the chair you're sitting in. Slide your buttocks off the edge of the chair and lower your body as far as you comfortably can by bending your arms. Return to the straight-arm position. Do as many dips as you can slowly and smoothly. Rest for one to two minutes, then repeat the exercise.

*Chin-ups.* This rather strenuous exercise should be approached respectfully. If possible, start with a firmly secured horizontal bar that you can barely grasp while standing flat-footed. With hands about shoulder-width apart and palms forward, grasp the bar firmly. Using a jumping motion to get you started, pull yourself upward until the level of your chin is slightly higher than that of the bar. Hang there for about five seconds, then slowly lower yourself. Check to see if you can pull up without resorting to a jumping motion. If so, do as many chin-ups as you can, rest for a minute or two, then repeat. If you can't chin-up without jumping, continue using the jump-and-hang method, lowering yourself slowly each time. Do as many of these as you can, rest, and repeat.

As in all exercises, make sure that you have warmed up with fairly vigorous movements before beginning. A reminder: it's not necessary to stretch just before exercising, but it is important to stay flexible at all times by stretching at least five times a week. The ITP Kata provides such stretches and warms you up before the stretches begin. Never stretch strenuously without warming up first. If you wish to make stretching a part of your exercise routine, it's best to stretch *after* exercising. Strenuous stretching with a cold body can cause injuries. Again—start slowly. Pay attention to the needs of your body. Use common sense.

### The Ultimate Physical Trainer

Most of all, don't forget to appreciate the miracle of the human body in motion. No matter what its present state of conditioning, this body is the culmination of an incredible evolutionary journey, the repository of the experience of aeons, the harbinger of adventures yet to come. We have suggested that you be sensible, take prudent precautions. We also know that life itself is risk, always has been, and always will be. Therefore, we respect your right to cross boundaries, to surpass limits, to take with a clear heart and mind the inevitable risks of transformation. The precautions are there to further the adventure, the strenuous training to further the joy. The ultimate physical trainer is not the man or woman with the clipboard, but the delight that resides in your own body, waiting for you to summon it forth.

# TEN

# *Food for Transformation*

So much has been written on what we should or shouldn't eat that we hesitate to add even one more line on this subject. Note the almost prurient gleam in the eyes of those around the table when someone reveals that he or she has embarked on a new diet. Consider how many dinner parties have been entirely devoted not just to eating but to talking about eating. And why not? Food is as basic as anything in our lives. We imagine our hunting and gathering forebears sitting around the campfire late into the night discussing the day's harvest of plants in its every particular and spinning ravenous fantasies about the results of the next successful hunt. Food is life. Before words, there is hunger, the crying need for nutrition, a word that comes from "nurse," close kin to "nourish," which takes us back to the Latin *nutrix*, "to nurse," the Sanskrit *snauti*, "she drips, gives milk," and the Greek *naein*, "to flow."

But food is more than sustenance. It is the centerpiece of our holiest ceremonies, the primary instrument of bonding among family, friends, and tribe. It is a marker of status and class, an emblem of national and ethnic heritage, the stuff of sensual pleasure and primal disgust, a medium that delights our aesthetic sense and tempts us with addiction, a nourishing friend, an unrelenting saboteur. For most of human history and for a significant proportion of the world's population today, the problem has been too little food. In the advanced nations today, the problem is often too much.

And not just too much food, but the wrong kind. Our current high-fat, high-cholesterol, salty, sugary diet represents, in fact, a radical and unsuccessful experiment in human adaptation. We evolved our bodies in the hunting and gathering life. Researcher S. Boyd Eaton's analysis of 153 species of wild plant foods eaten by hunting and gathering Africans shows the average protein and fiber content to be much higher than in our plant foods. Hunter-gatherer sodium consumption is estimated at 690 milligrams daily, as compared to between 2,000 and 7,000 for present-day Americans. The fat content of the Bushman's diet was 21 percent (with a high ratio of polyunsaturates), compared to our 40 or so percent. The question: can an organism evolved to eat a low-fat diet safely adapt to a diet of 40 percent or more of fat? In the long run, probably not. The evidence comes from many sources, none more graphic than the fate of people in places such as Singapore who shifted from a low- to a high-fat diet in a very short period of time, only to see an explosive increase in the incidence of obesity, cancer, and heart disease. A steady high-fat diet, we feel, insults the body our species has evolved, not only threatening our health but dulling our minds and dragging down our spirits.

Still, we prescribe no specific diet, nor do we push for weight loss. In fact, we explicitly oppose the whole idea of "dieting." We do, however, recommend that everyone eat a healthy, balanced diet. The ITP commitment on the subject of food is quite simple: *We are conscious of everything we eat.* To be conscious means to pay attention, to be mindful, as you choose or prepare food and as you eat, and that you stay mindful of the aftereffects of the food eaten.

In both the 1992 and 1993 ITP classes, we offered participants information on the benefits of a low-fat diet, and in the 1993 class we measured the change in percentage of the participants' bodies composed of fat. This was done by means of caliper skin-fold tests on March 27, 1993, and again on November 13, 1993. After the first caliper test, eight class members and three of the teachers joined a health club for strength training. All of these people showed significant reductions in percent body fat, but so did many others who engaged in no strength training at all. What correlated best with reduced body fat, as it turned out, was the time spent doing aerobic exercise. During the seven-and-a-half-month period between March 27 and November 13, twenty-seven of the thirty ITP participants showed reductions in body fat. The class as a whole lost 122 pounds of fat and gained 66 pounds of lean body mass for an average fat loss of 12.6 percent and an average muscle gain of 2 percent, a notable achievement considering the fact that most class members were already in rather good shape. By and large, this bodily change was accomplished without the agonizing effort, the sense of deprivation, that goes along with dieting.

*We have a genius for overlooking openings to extraordinary life.*

M.M.

We chose loss in percentage of body fat as an affirmation in 1993 because it would give us a purely objective measurement of the program's effectiveness and also because a body with a low ratio of fat to muscle is such a crucial factor in overall health and vitality—as demonstrated clearly in research by Dr. William Evans and others (see chapter 9). Though overall weight loss was not particularly encouraged, some participants lost significant amounts of weight, it seems, despite themselves. Simply by being conscious of what they were eating, many participants found their nutritional preferences gradually shifting away from foods high in fat and sugar. It's important here to stress that far from pushing our ITP participants to change their diets, we simply provided information on the benefits of conscious, balanced eating.

Over the years, we have discovered that specific diets, especially those promising quick weight loss, can be part of the problem rather than the solution. A panel of experts convened by the National Institutes of Health Nutrition Coordinating Committee concluded that when people diet, "there is a strong tendency to regain weight, with as much as two-thirds of the weight loss regained within one year of completing the program, and almost all by five years." Nor is fasting the solution to the problem of obesity. As an occasional spiritual practice, it might have its value, but as a weight-loss strategy, it can be disappointing, if not disastrous. When you deprive the body of food, it interprets this as stress and immediately goes into action to deposit fat while decreasing the utilization of stored fat. To eat with full awareness can be, in itself, a sacramental act.

At the end of the 1993 cycle, we asked our participants to rate the healthfulness of their diet on a scale of 0 to 10 especially in terms of

**The Fruits of Conscious Eating**

avoiding a high-fat content. They came up with a respectable average of 7.10. While the benefits of a diet low in fat were presented merely as something to bear in mind, being conscious of everything eaten was a definite commitment, and the participants' adherence to this commitment was reflected in the extremely high average response of 8.83 to the following question: "Over the last seven days, how conscious have you been of what you have eaten on a scale of zero to ten, with zero being totally unconscious and ten being totally conscious?"

*Metanormal capacities typically emerge from normal abilities that have been developed through life-encompassing practice.*

M.M.

Both the healthfulness of the participants' diet, and their consciousness of what they ate turned out to have a strong statistical relationship to their success in achieving Affirmation Four, "My entire body is balanced, vital, and healthy." Of the two, however, only the response involving consciousness was also related in a statistically significant way with their success in achieving Affirmations One (normal), Three, (metanormal), and Four ("balanced, vital, and healthy") *combined*. Surprisingly, neither of the questions regarding food correlated to a statistically significant degree to Affirmation Two (the participants' success in reducing their percentage of body fat). Only two factors (as noted earlier) could be significantly related to that affirmation: the average number of minutes of aerobic exercise a week and regularity of class attendance (see Appendix B).

Statistics can be useful, but are not the last word; we know of several people in the program whose success in reducing percentage of body fat must have had some relation with low-fat eating. The fact that most of our participants were quite fit to start out with was another factor in this equation. Low-fat eating would probably have a significant impact on reducing the percentage of body fat of any group whose members were overweight. Even then, however, aerobic exercise would doubtless play a major role.

## WEIGHT LOSS AS A SIDE EFFECT

Though overall weight loss was not particularly encouraged, some class members lost significant amounts of weight, almost it seemed, despite themselves. The most striking case was that of Karen Wilson, whose experience during a mass shooting at her law firm was described in chapter 2. Karen turned to conscious, low-fat eating when she first signed on for Cycle 93, two months before the class began in February 1993. At that time, she weighed 138 at a height of 5 foot 5. When the class ended on November 28, she weighed 108.

"Interestingly enough," Karen explained, "my goal was not to lose weight. It was to lose body fat and to get healthy. That was the one thought in my mind all the time. I was really conscious of what I ate. I've had moments of unconsciously eating things, but I'm just more aware of everything I eat. It's not to say I don't sometimes make conscious choices to eat things that are not good for me—like I ate a lot of fudge at Christmas time. But it was a conscious choice, and I used to do kind of mindless eating, nervous eating, snacking on something when I wasn't particularly hungry. My whole relationship to food is something I think is permanently changed due to this class."

At first, Karen found giving up fat hard but soon began enjoying her new way of eating. "A perfect example is, this morning I went to breakfast with a friend and she had eggs Benedict, and looking at that hollandaise sauce on her plate was almost too much for me. It looked terrible. I know how hollandaise sauce tastes. It's just too rich. I can't eat things like that anymore. I have no desire to eat things like that. You change in what appeals to you—what sounds good, what looks good."

Karen followed the program faithfully, doing the Kata five times a week, rarely missing her aerobic exercise. Losing thirty pounds, she insisted, was "really effortless."

## A Fundamental Expression of our Embodiment

We recommend that you eat no fast food. But if, for some reason, you must, eat even that with full awareness. Better to eat slowly, chewing thoroughly, savoring every mouthful. Better to cherish the pure magnificence of fruits and vegetables when they are in season—the color, the texture, the flavor, the subtle yet captivating smell. Better to watch the steam curling up from fresh-baked salmon. Better to create rituals before beginning to eat, with soft music, candlelight.

Let us say it again: we are less concerned with the precise content of your diet than with the quality of your food consciousness.

Finally, how we eat, just as is the case with how we exercise, stands as a fundamental expression of our embodiment and is thus important to our practice, not merely for the benefits it might bring but *for its own sake*. To eat with full awareness turns us toward a diet that is both good and good for us. It rejoins us with the matrix of our existence and can inspire us with thanksgiving for the everyday wonder of food, the everlasting miracle of the life we are given.

# ELEVEN

# The Body as Teacher

There is a profound wisdom in the body, in the pulsing of the blood, the rhythm of the breath, the turning of the joints. Once we are aware of its subtle power, the body becomes a sensitive antenna for tuning into nature and other people. It can serve as a metaphor for every human thought, emotion, and action. It is a royal road to the unconscious. It is a small, handy model of the universe. All the books, computers, and electronic networks in the world contain only a miniscule fraction of the information it takes to create one human body.

It is also a master teacher. In our ITP practice, we offer exercises that call upon this teacher not only to show us how to live a more balanced, vital, and healthy life but also to point the way toward the next stage of human evolution. As previously pointed out, we see body, mind, heart, and soul as coequal manifestations of the human essence. But where deep down human change is concerned, there is no more effective teacher than the body. In a culture that has traditionally downgraded the flesh and routinely characterized it as a threat to the workings of the mind, such a statement might seem strange. But far from opposing the mind, the body reflects and is reflected by it with amazing fidelity.

Our posture, for example, stands as one of the most comprehensive statements we can make about ourselves. To stand more erectly is to change our relationship with the world. When energy is out of balance in the body there is probably some corresponding imbalance in the psyche. By increasing bodily awareness, by tuning in to the fascinating information the body is continually broadcasting to mind, heart, and soul, we can increase awareness of the world through every domain of our existence and create a harmonious relationship between our many parts. We can also follow the body's guidance in developing new ways of dealing with everyday problems and, beyond that, in developing extraordinary capacities.

The following exercises are drawn from Leonard Energy Training (LET), a discipline inspired by the sophisticated martial art of aikido, along with Western psychology and physical theory. In this chapter, we present a selection of LET exercises. They are not designed to be done on a daily or weekly basis but rather to be experienced once, then repeated whenever desired. In them, you will practice new ways of being in the world and perhaps discover remarkable capabilities you didn't know you had.

## Balancing and Centering

This essential exercise, an amplification of the GRACE checklist that begins the ITP Kata (see chapter 6), aims not at achieving perfect balance but rather discovering just how you are off balance in every particular. With practice, you can bring your bodily balance into a more harmonious state that will be reflected in every aspect of your life.

*Balanced* means simply that the weight and energy of the body is distributed evenly, right and left, forward and back, all the way from the head to the toes. *Centered* means that body awareness is focused primarily in the center of the abdomen rather than, say, the head or shoulders, and also that movement is initiated from that center.

For most of us top-heavy, forward-pushing Westerners, something as simple as focusing our attention on the abdomen can bring extraordinary results. During a moment of crisis, for example, just touching yourself lightly at a point on the abdomen an inch or two below the navel can alter your attitude and your ability to deal with whatever situation you face.

Try this: Stand normally and draw your attention to the top of your body by tapping yourself a couple of times on the forehead.

Then have a partner push you from behind at the shoulder blades just hard enough to make you lose your balance and take a step forward. Next, stand exactly the same way and draw your attention to your center by tapping yourself a couple of times about an inch or two below the navel. Then have your partner push you with exactly the same force as before. Most people find they are more stable with their attention on their centers.

And not just physically. To go into a tense, adversarial situation with body awareness concentrated in head, shoulders, and upper chest is almost certain to produce a different outcome than would be the case if you went into the same situation with attention on the abdomen. The former is more likely to lead to a heated, ineffectual exchange of words and an escalation of the conflict, while the latter tends to bring calm confidence and the power to effect a satisfactory resolution. Again, this might seem strange to those who are not accustomed to dealing with bodily awareness, but the difference in outcome is striking. Try it for yourself.

Eastern martial arts have long stressed the practice of being balanced and centered and the influence of the physical on the psychological. Note the correspondence between a person's physical stance and his or her performance in various nonphysical activities. In our experience, a person who habitually stands and walks with head and shoulders thrust forward is also likely to get ahead of himself or herself in thinking and talking, even in something as cerebral as authoring a technical paper. Such a person tends to come to conclusions without adequate background and backup material. The match between the physical and the cerebral is often uncanny. Correcting your stance through long-term practice, as we have said, can have a powerful effect on every aspect of your life.

You'll need someone to read the following instructions while one or more people go through the balancing and centering procedure. Read slowly and clearly, pausing for a while wherever there are ellipses:

"Please stand with your feet slightly farther apart than your shoulders, eyes open, knees not locked and not bent, trunk upright, arms relaxed by your sides. . . . Now take the fingers of your right hand and touch them to a spot an inch or two below your navel. Press firmly, toward the center of your abdomen. . . . Now drop your right hand to your side. . . . Let yourself breathe normally. Let the breath move downward through your body as if it were going di-

rectly to your center. Let your abdomen expand with the incoming
breath, from the center outward to the front, to the rear, to the sides
of the pelvis, to the floor of the pelvis. . . .

"As your breathing continues in a relaxed manner, lift your arms
in front of you, with the wrists limp. Shake your hands so hard that
your whole body vibrates. . . . Now lower your arms to your sides. As
soon as they touch your legs, let them start rising very slowly, directly in front of you, as if you were standing up to your neck in
warm, salty water and your arms were floating to the surface. As the
arms rise, lower your body by bending the knees slightly. Let the
hands hang loosely, palms down, just as they would if floating in
warm water. Keep the trunk upright. When your arms reach the
horizontal, put the palms forward into the position you would use if
gently pushing a beach ball on the surface of the water. Shoulders relaxed. Sweep the arms from left to right and right to left as if you
could sense or 'see' things around you through your open palms. . . .

"Now shake out your hands and repeat the process. . . . Lower
your arms to your sides and let them float up again. As the arms rise,
the body slightly lowers. Knees bent very slightly, trunk upright.
Now put the palms forward and sweep your arms from side to side as
if sensing the world through your palms. . . .

"All right. Drop your hands, and this time leave them hanging
by your sides naturally, in a totally relaxed manner. . . . Please close
your eyes. Knees not locked and not bent. Check to see if your
weight is balanced evenly between your right and left foot. Shift
your weight very slightly from side to side, fine-tuning your balance. . . . Now check to see if your weight is balanced evenly between
the heels and balls of your feet. . . . Knees not locked and not
bent. . . . Please leave your eyes closed and shift to a more comfortable position any time you wish. . . . Now move your head forward
and backward to find the point at which it can be balanced upright
on your spine with the least muscular effort. Be sensitive, as if you
were fine-tuning a distant station on your radio. . . .

"Take a moment to relax your jaw . . . your tongue . . . your eyelids . . . the muscles around your eyes . . . your forehead, temples,
scalp . . . the back of your neck. . . .

"Now, with a sharp intake of breath, raise and tighten your
shoulders. . . . As you exhale, let your shoulders drop and relax completely. They are not slumping forward but melting straight downward, like soft, warm butter. With each outgoing breath, let them

melt a little farther. . . . Let that same melting sensation move down your shoulder blades . . . your arms . . . your rib cage . . . down to your diaphragm. . . . Let all your internal organs rest, relax, soften. . . . And now the lower pelvic region: let that relax, too. Release all tension. With each outgoing breath, let go a bit more. . . . Let the melting, relaxing sensation move down your legs to your feet. . . . Feel your feet warming the floor and the floor warming your feet. Sense the secure embrace of gravity that holds you to the earth and holds the earth to you. . . .

"Now consider the back half of your body. What if you could sense what is behind you? What would that be like? What if you had sensors, or 'eyes,' in the small of your back? . . . At the back of your neck? . . . At the back of your knees? . . . With your eyes closed, can you get the general *feeling* of what is behind you? . . .

"Now send a beam of awareness throughout your entire body, seeking out any area that might be tense or rigid or numb. Illuminate that area, focus on it. Sometimes awareness alone takes care of these problems. . . .

"Once more, concentrate on your breathing. . . . Be aware of the rhythm. . . . Now, in rhythm with one of the incoming breaths, let your eyes open. Don't look at any one thing in particular, just let the world come in. We call this the soft-eyed configuration, seeing the periphery just as well as what is directly in front of you. . . . With eyes soft, walk around slowly, maintaining the relaxed and balanced state you've achieved. . . . Let your physical center be your center of awareness. . . . See if things look and feel different to you after this exercise."

As you go through the rest of the day, you might re-create the centering and balancing process at various times. After practice, it takes only a few seconds. Bear in mind that the body can be considered a metaphor for everything else. Your relationships, your work, your fitness activities, your entire life can be centered and balanced. If you should be knocked off center in one way or another, there is always the possibility—if you can stay aware—of returning to the balanced and centered condition at an even deeper level.

### The Power of Relaxation: A Change of Context

This exercise, derived from the art of aikido, demonstrates the extraordinary human power made possible through a change of con-

*There are endless ways to turn an impulse into an exercise.*
M.M.

text. The word *context* comes from two Latin roots: *con*, with or together, and *texere*, to weave (as in *textile*). In this light, a context is not
a passive container for your experience but rather an active process.
When you change the way you weave your experiences together,
some sort of transformation may well occur.

Start by standing and extending one arm to a horizontal position. Either arm will do, but let's say it's the left arm this time. The
hand should be open with the fingers spread and the thumb pointing
straight up. Have a partner stand at the left of your arm and bend it
at the elbow by pressing *up* at your wrist and *down* at your elbow.
Don't resist. Note that this exercise involves bending the arm at the
elbow, not the shoulder.

Now that your partner has practiced bending your arm without
any resistance on your part, you'll try two radically different ways
of making your arm strong and resilient. After each of these, your
partner will attempt to bend your arm at the elbow, adding force
gradually. Your partner should not add so much force that a struggle
ensues. Bear in mind that this is not a contest but a *comparison* of two
different ways of being powerful. The point is to see how much effort is required to keep the arm straight under pressure.

*The power of relaxation*

***The first way.***  Hold your arm rigidly straight. Use your muscles to keep your arm from being bent. Resist. Fight *against* your partner's pressure. Have your partner gradually apply force in an attempt to bend your arm. Your arm might bend or it might not. In either case, note how much effort you exerted in the process. Perhaps even more important, note how you feel about this experience.

***The change of context.***  Take a balanced and centered stance and let your arm rise to the same horizontal position as before. This time, sense the aliveness of your arm and the energy flowing from your shoulder to your fingertips. Now visualize or feel your arm as part of a powerful laser beam that starts an infinite distance behind you, then extends through your arm and out past your fingertips, through any walls or other objects in front of you, across the horizon and to the ends of the universe. This beam is larger than your arm, and your arm is a part of it. Your arm is not rigid or tense. In fact, it is quite re-laxed. But remember that being relaxed is not being limp. Your arm is full of life and energy. Assume that if anyone tried to bend your arm, the beam would become even more powerful and penetrating, and your arm, without effort, would become more powerful.

Now have your partner gradually apply exactly the same amount of force as before—or perhaps even more—in an attempt to bend your arm. Note how much effort you expended in this case. How do you feel about this experience? The overwhelming majority of peo-ple who have tried this exercise find the second way, the "energy arm," significantly more powerful and resilient than the first way, the "resistance arm." Electromyographic measurements of the electrical activity in the muscles indicate that this subjective judgment is cor-rect. The energy arm might give a little, but is far less likely to col-lapse than the resistance arm.

The implications for physical performance are obvious: relax-ation is essential to the full expression of power. And if we take the body as a metaphor for other aspects of our lives, the implications are even more significant. Just think what kind of world it would be if we all realized we could be powerful in everything we do without being rigid and resistant. Take the force on your arm as any problem in your life, then note that in resisting it you were fighting *against* the pressure to bend your arm, and thus were giving power to the problem. In changing context, you focused on your own power by concentrating on your center, while extending your attention *beyond* the problem in sending a beam to the ends of the universe. Try using this change of context in dealing with every problem, physical or nonphysical, that you encounter.

### TAKING THE HIT AS A GIFT

Rarely have we received guidance on dealing with life's sudden hits, those misfortunes that come without warning. This exercise will allow you to experience an effective way of dealing with them. More than that, it will show you how to *gain* energy from negative happenings, how to turn a hit into a gift, perhaps even a life-transforming experience.

Unexpected blows come in many varieties, from the merely bothersome to the profound. Say you own an antique gold watch handed down from a grandparent, a watch you intend to bequeath to one of your grandchildren. One day, on a boat, you take the watch out to show to a friend; it slips from your hand and drops into deep water. Or say you and your spouse are driving to a wedding along a lonely road, running a little late. Suddenly there is a loud sound and your car lurches to a halt; a tire has blown out. Or say you've worked long and hard to complete a report for your supervisor. You give it to her on Friday afternoon. On Monday morning, she walks into your office holding the report. You smile inwardly, anticipating praise. She throws it on your desk: "This is chaos. It makes no sense at all." Or say your spouse comes home one day wearing a strange, pained expression. "I haven't had the nerve to tell you before, but I have to tell you now that I've been having an affair with your best friend."

Our most common responses to such unfortunate happenings tend to make things worse:

***Immediate counterattack. Fighting back reflexively.*** "Whad'ya mean 'chaos'? This is a damned good report!" Or you might get out of the disabled car and kick the offending tire. Such responses generally only strengthen and solidify the problem.

***Whining, playing the victim's role.*** "Oh no! Not *again!* Why do things like this always happen to me?" The victim's role is not only unattractive, it's self-defeating, inviting misfortune without redemption, forfeiting all chances of an eventual positive outcome.

***Denial.*** "This doesn't bother me. I can handle it. I don't feel a thing." While it's tempting to steel yourself against the vicissitudes of life, to turn off or control your feelings, this path is a particularly dangerous one. If you practice turning off your feelings long enough, you might get too good at it. You might become so insensitive that you honestly don't have the faintest idea that, for instance, you're hurting your young daughter's feelings by laughing at one of her sincere questions; you have to be aware of your own feelings to be aware of others' feelings. What's more, as numerous studies suggest, blocked emotions can be unhealthy for the heart and the rest of the body.

There are better ways. We propose a response to sudden hits that involves fully experiencing and acknowledging strong feelings and using the energy of those feelings to handle the situation at hand—with plenty of power left over for further good works. In the following exercise, you'll have your partner create a representation of a sudden hit by sneaking up behind you, grabbing your wrist, and shouting. You need only enough impact to make you jump, to lose

*Taking the hit as a gift*

your center. So let your partner know how jumpy you are; maybe you'll need only a very mild startle to do the job.

Start by standing with feet about as far apart as the width of your shoulders, eyes open and soft. Balance and center. When you're ready, let your arms swing out from the sides of your body to a forty-five-degree angle. This is your partner's signal to walk up stealthily behind you and grab either your right or left wrist with both of his or her hands while simultaneously giving a shout. The grab should be sudden and firm, but *should not pull you off balance in any direction.* Your partner should continue to hold your wrist firmly while you process the experience.

Be totally aware of how the sudden hit affected you. Speaking aloud in a clear voice, describe exactly what is going on within you. Specify exactly where in your body each feeling or sensation is located. Don't look at your partner as you speak. Resist the temptation to point the finger of your free hand at different parts of your body. Use words only and be as specific as possible. For example: "When you grabbed me, I jumped and blinked both eyes. My heart seemed to jump up into my throat. Now my throat feels a little dry. I can feel the pressure of your hands on my right wrist. My left shoulder is a little high. My abdomen feels tight. My breathing is shallower than usual."

Keep speaking until you have nothing more to say. At this point, you might note that most of the conditions you've described have melted away. Many people discover that merely becoming aware of an imbalance tends to correct it.

The second part of the exercise requires a change of context. Consider the fact that this sudden shock, by startling you and knocking you off center, has *added energy* to your body and your psyche. In acknowledging and specifying your feelings, you've avoided fighting back reflexively, whining about your fate, or denying your feelings. Your adrenal glands have shot a hormonal cocktail into your bloodstream. As a result of being startled, your entire nervous system has come to the alert. You've been shaken out of whatever lethargy might have previously held you in check. Now you can choose what positive uses you wish to make of the extra energy that is yours to use.

Take a series of deep breaths. Move up and down rhythmically by bending and unbending your knees. Become aware of the extra energy you now possess. Even the tight grip on your wrist is giving

*Even from misfortune, great power can flow into you.*
G.L.

you energy. Begin moving around with a feeling of power. Your partner may be having trouble holding you. In any case, ask your partner to release your wrist and walk around the room expansively, arms open. Ask yourself if you have more energy now than when you started the exercise.

Being grabbed by the wrist is not, of course, the same as being confronted by some unexpected blow in your life. But this exercise guides you toward an alternative way of dealing with sudden hits of many types and many degrees of severity. Say your supervisor throws your report on your desk and says, "This is chaos!" You might try not shouting back, "What do you mean, 'chaos'? This is a damned good report. What's more—" That might well make matters worse. Don't whine and complain; playing the victim is, in many ways, a losing game. Most of all, don't deny your feelings. Say to yourself, for example, "Boy, I felt that like a blow to the solar plexis. My mouth feels dry. I feel something like anger throbbing at my temples and in the back of my head." Or, if you know your supervisor well enough and have established a certain openness in the expression of feelings, you might even speak your feelings aloud. Just *your* feelings. Don't try to lay blame on the supervisor. Then consider the possibility that this sudden blow has given you the energy with which you and your supervisor, working together, can come up with an even better report. And note how energized you feel. This extra energy can be put to use in many ways.

The particulars of responding to each sudden hit vary, but the pattern is always the same: Fully experience and acknowledge your feelings by localizing them in your body. Be aware of the infusion of extra energy caused by the hit. Put this energy to use for some positive purpose.

## BLENDING: AN ALTERNATIVE WAY OF DEALING WITH VERBAL ATTACKS

*"What do you do when somebody pushes you?"*

George Leonard has asked this question to various groups, totaling some fifty thousand individuals. In every case, the first answer has been, "Push back." This response to an attack, whether physical or verbal, is deeply ingrained in present-day cultures; Leonard has heard "Push back" in several languages. The problem is, such a response leads to a very limited number of outcomes—win, lose, or stalemate—none of which is ideal. If you win, someone else loses. Losing doesn't feel very good. And a stalemate is a big waste of time. The exercise described here introduces you to a change of context, an alternative response to a verbal attack that greatly multiplies your options.

A note of caution and clarification. We are not teaching physical self-defense here. Blending with physical attacks, a skill most highly developed in the art of aikido, takes months or years to learn. Verbal blending also takes practice to perfect, but it can be used from the very beginning. In this exercise, you'll have an opportunity to get the *feel* of blending through bodily movement under pressure. This physical experience will teach you the principles of verbal blending in a more immediate and dramatic fashion than would be possible using words alone.

To do the exercise, you'll need a partner to play the part of an attacker. Start by standing with your right foot about eight to ten inches directly in front of the left. Your left foot is turned out to the left at a forty-five-degree angle. Both feet are planted firmly on the

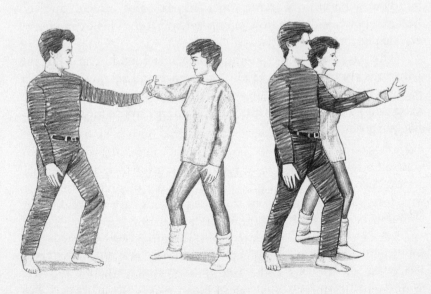

*Blending*

ground. You and the person playing the part of the attacker are standing a few feet apart, facing one another.

Extend your right arm straight out directly in front of you, toward your attacker, with fist clenched, thumb up. Now bend your right arm until the forearm is at a ninety-degree angle to the upper arm, level and directly in front of you. Your attacker then comes forward, grasps your right wrist with his or her left hand and pushes directly toward you. Push back. Don't overdo the struggle that ensues from this "push–push back" mode of dealing with an attack. Just push back long enough to get the feel of it. Recall an episode of verbal sparring in your life when push–push back was the guiding rule. Note its similarity to this physical struggle.

The attacker releases your wrist and steps back. Take the same stance and arm position as before, but this time, instead of making a fist, leave your right hand open. Briefly balance and center. Feel the energy flowing through your arm and out of your fingers. Once again, the attacker comes toward you, grasps your right wrist with his or her left hand, and pushes directly toward you. Don't push back. Instead, move slightly toward the attacker and turn to the left, rotating in place as the attacker takes one or two more steps forward, until you are facing in the same direction as the attacker, keeping your arm and hand alive and full of energy. At this point, both of you stop so that you can experience your new situation.

What has happened? You might say that the attack has been diffused or simply that you and your attacker are now lined up in the same direction. But the important point is that you are now seeing the situation from your attacker's viewpoint—*without losing your own.* Consider how different this feels compared to the situation when you were facing your attacker, struggling to push back harder than he or she was pushing you. Note that by blending, you've given yourself a few moments to decide on how to further deal with the attack. Also note that you now have many options rather than just win, lose, or stalemate. From this position, it's easy to break from your attacker's grasp and take leave of the situation or to embrace the attacker or to turn the attack to a new direction or even to strike a winning blow. Blending is not a passive act. It is not "giving in." It is seeing the situation from the attacker's viewpoint, then acting appropriately, bearing in mind that a blend makes reconciliation not only possible but likely.

In the martial arts, the blend stands as an extremely powerful move. Verbally, it is perhaps even more powerful, not only diffusing the force of an attack but often leading to harmonious agreement. As an example, let's say a futurist has made a speech about a visionary school of the twenty-first century where much of the teaching is accomplished through advanced technology. During the question period, an aggressive young man launches a verbal attack. Here we compare two ways of responding:

1. *Push–push back. Aggressive young man rises to his feet with a wicked grin.* "That was a nice little scenario you gave us, but like most futurism it's totally impractical. Where would you get the money to pay for all that technology?"

"Well—" *Speaker pauses, then responds with lofty sarcasm.* "I guess we'd get it where we get all those generous funds we currently devote to our younger generation. Seriously, we could fund a great deal of advanced technology with the money we now spend dealing with the human failures produced by present antiquated educational methods."

"Just a minute! Not so fast!" *Aggressive young man's voice rises.* "The kind of computer power needed for your scenario would cost at least $100,000 for each school and would call for a level of artificial intelligence that doesn't now exist. I have to disagree with you. Your scenario is totally unrealistic."

*Speaker tries to control anger.* "I assume you're not familiar with the work of Ned Morosco at Massachusetts Institute of Technology. He's already working with prototypes that can do just about everything I've outlined. In any case, what's keeping us from a better future isn't lack of money. It's lack of vision. If the naysayers take over, we just as well give it up. Next question."

*The aggressive young man shakes his head with derision as he sits down. The speaker has "won" but doesn't feel very good. The audience has had its interest piqued by the interchange, but some of its members are embarrassed and a few feel bad for the young man.*

2. *Blending. Aggressive young man rises to his feet with a wicked grin.* "That was a nice little scenario you gave us, but like most futurism it's totally impractical. Where would you get the money to pay for all that technology?"

*Speaker nods thoughtfully.* "That's a good question. I worry about that myself. What you're saying is that new technology is very expensive."

"Yeah, right. And not only that, the computer capability you're talking about doesn't exist yet—and we're not even near getting there."

"Yes, that's true too. I hear what you're saying."

"But, you know—" (*Young man no longer seems aggressive.*) "You know, computers keep getting cheaper all the time. And the increase in memory capacity and speed is exponential."

"Right. I've heard that a generation in computer technology is now defined as two and a half or three years."

"Well, maybe it could happen—if we had the will to do it."

"Right. If we had the will. I really appreciate your comments." *The young man smiles as he takes his seat.*

The first interchange is purely imaginary; it never happened. The second took place during a lecture on education by George Leonard at a large western university. Blending doesn't always work this neatly, with the attacker coming over to the blender's side—*but it often does.* During a book promotion tour, one of the authors went on a radio show as the guest of a man known as the most abrasive talk show host in New York. The program began with a particularly virulent attack, impuning the author's character and painting him as a threat to society. After an hour of blending, the situation couldn't have been more different. Near the end of the show—with the producer in the control room tearing at his hair in frustration—the host and the author were talking with genuine warmth and understanding. The host ended the show by reading the last page of the author's book, with feeling. People who heard the program characterized the shift in the host's attitude as "unbelievable," "miraculous." It was not that he had been manipulated. He had been truly heard and understood, and from that he was able to reveal a deeper, truer persona than the one required for contentious commercialism.

We have said more than once that long-term change takes long-term practice, but if there is an exception to prove the rule, blending might qualify. Though it takes practice to master the art, even unskilled blending rather than pushing back can produce an immediate change in outcome. But there are some provisos and guidelines:

Blending is presented here as an option, not a one-size-fits-all solution. There are some situations best dealt with through grappling. In a sense, blending is *too* powerful. To use it invariably with your spouse and children, for example, can drive them crazy. ("Mom, will you *stop* blending with me all the time?") And then there are some attacks so destructive, so evil, if you will, that they must be quickly struck down. But even in the worst situations, even in war, it's good to be able to view the situation from the attacker's viewpoint.

For a blend to be successful, you should be psychologically balanced and centered, and this means being physically balanced and centered. It's very hard if not impossible to blend if your energy is concentrated in your head and upper chest. To remind yourself to stay balanced and centered while blending, touch your physical center.

Blending doesn't work if done insincerely, just as a strategy. You must come around wholeheartedly to view the situation from the attacker's viewpoint. Again, this doesn't mean giving up your viewpoint. As you start to blend verbally, imagine turning all the way around physically to the attacker's viewpoint rather than turning only part of the way.

Continue practicing this exercise to get the feeling of wholehearted blending. Do it left-handed as well as right-handed. When you feel familiar with the physical exercise, add a verbal attack to the physical. Have your partner verbally attack some position you hold at the same time he or she grasps your wrist and pushes. Blend verbally as you turn. Continue blending verbally as you stand viewing the situation physically from your attacker's viewpoint.

We are by no means suggesting that you do anything to provoke a real-life confrontation just so you can check out the blending option. But if by chance you are attacked verbally, give it a try.

## The Crystalline State

This exercise offers you an opportunity to perceive the world with the vivid here and now clarity common to many mystical and other exalted experiences. In the crystalline state, there is no expectation nor any prejudgment. Concentration on the past and future gives way to primary focus on the present. Action taken while in the crystalline state is not *considered* action but rather *appropriate* action. When fully achieved, this state permits awareness of what might be called the perfect rhythm that always exists at the heart of your being. Awareness of this rhythm can come upon you spontaneously. It can arise during meditation. Most people have experienced a few moments or hours or even days during which it seems that nothing can go wrong, that all things are somehow connected, that what is most commonplace is also most wonderous. No set of instructions can guarantee that you will arrive at such a state. The following procedure is offered merely as a guide. Your own intentionality is the key ingredient.

Sit comfortably, either in meditation position on a cushion on the floor or in a straight-backed chair. Balance and center. Using soft vision, create an imaginary ball about the size of a volleyball between your hands. Hold the ball gently. Sense its surface by moving your hands slightly together in a rhythmic manner. Let the ball become

*The crystalline state*

real in your imagination. Check if you can *feel* where its surface begins as you move your hands in and out.

Continuing to palpate the ball, think of your most pressing personal problem. *Put this problem in the ball*. Focus your eyes on the problem. Let it take its own shape and texture and color. What does the problem look like now? Does it move? What part of the ball does it occupy?

Ask yourself whether you're willing to give up that problem for the next twenty or thirty minutes (or for however long you want to extend the period). Are you willing to let go of the problem completely for at least this long? Assure yourself that you can get it back when the exercise is finished, if you so desire. (Your problems are important aspects of your ego. In this case, in fact, this particular problem might be said to represent your ego.)

Now, if you're really willing to give up your problem for this next period of time, press the ball with the problem in it down into the floor. Let it sink into the earth. The earth will serve as a bank; you can always recover the problem later.

Shake out your hands. Balance and center. Again create a ball between your hands. The ball is as pure and clear as a crystal. Focus your eyes on its center, allowing the background to go out of focus. Continue "feeling" the ball by moving your hands slightly in and out. You might find it hard to stay focused on "nothing," but keep bringing your focus back to that central point. Continue this practice for about five minutes.

During this period, consider that the crystalline state, now represented by the ball, contains no expectations and no prejudgment. It exists in the vibrancy of the present moment. In this state, what you experience is neither "good" nor "bad," neither "successful" nor "unsuccessful." It just *is*. You experience the world as a young child would: as if for the first time.

After five minutes or so of concentration have passed, ask yourself, "Am I willing to live during this next period of time entirely in the present, without expectation or prejudgment? If the answer that comes from your heart is no, throw the ball away and, if you so desire, take back your problem from the earth. If your heart's answer is yes, however, press the ball into your body at the point of your physical center. This act represents your induction into the crystalline state. Feel the ball expand inside you and spread to fill your whole being.

In the crystalline state now, rise and walk around, experiencing familiar things as if for the first time—a chair, a table, a painting, a flower, a tree. Approach each experience without expectation or prejudgment. Go to a mirror and look at yourself from the intense clarity of the present moment. Maybe you can arrange to meet a friend, a loved one, or a stranger while in this state. If so, there need be nothing out of the ordinary about your external appearance and actions; the crystalline state entails *appropriate* action, and it is appropriate to meet another person in a relaxed and natural manner. Your own experience during the meeting, however, could well be transformed, and this transformation might reveal itself in the essential quality of the relationship. For example, having dropped at least a portion of the dubious armor of prejudgment, you might feel a certain compassion and understanding rather than suspicion or dismissal, thus opening a new level of dialogue.

Whenever you wish, you can return to the state we consider "normal." Remember that your pressing personal problem is still there for you to retrieve and return to your consciousness, if you so desire. The crystalline state is an *alternative* mode of being. To offer it is not to denigrate other modes. The point is that to be able to move into the crystalline state at will, eventually without the induction procedure presented here, is to enjoy the possibility of a richer, more fascinating, more humane life.

## TUNING IN

This exercise and the two that follow offer you the possibility of sampling metanormal sensing. This one requires a partner. You and your partner sit facing each other in the meditation position on cushions or in straight-backed chairs, so close that your knees touch. Both you and your partner should balance and center, then go into the crystalline state. Place your hands on your knees, palms up, and have your partner place his or her hands, palms down, into yours. Both of you now close your eyes.

At this point, simply assume that your partner's bodily states are known to you at some deep level, and that, in fact, you can feel in *your* body every bodily state your partner feels. Let your body be a sensitive antenna that is tuned in to your partner's body. Wait a few minutes, then, if you feel a tightness in your own neck, say aloud to your partner, "There's a tightness in your neck. See if you can relax it." Keep tuning in. If you should feel your neck relaxing, say aloud, "Good, your neck is relaxing now." Keep tuning in by mentally scanning your own body for anything out of the ordinary. Report anything you feel to your partner as if the condition exists in his or her body.

After all possible corrections have been made, start working on *positive* change, on creating a sense of glowing awareness and aliveness in your partner's body. Again, use feelings in your own body as a guide. For example, "Your head feels full of life and energy, but the aliveness seems to stop at your neck, leaving your body rather numb. See if you can let the energy flow downward from your head into your body." Keep tuning in. When you feel a change in your own body, report it as a change in your partner's body. "Good. Now the energy has flowed through your neck as far as your heart. See if you can let it flow downward and fill your whole body."

Continue giving instructions in this manner until your own body feels relaxed, alive, and glowing. Then, along with your partner, take a few deep breaths, shift your weight, stretch, and open your eyes. Compare notes. Which of your instructions were on target? Which were meaningful and useful? Now change roles and repeat the exercise.

## TOUCHING THE WORLD

The primary purpose of this exercise is to make it possible for you to sense a new connectedness with the world. Start by doing it at a location from which you can see a tree or shrub. Briefly balance and center yourself. Bear in mind that in an expanding universe every point can serve as its center. Look in the general direction of the tree with soft eyes, then let your eyes focus on a particular leaf. With the index finger extended, let your left hand rise and point directly at that leaf. The arm and shoulder should be relaxed. Your assumption here is that some aspect of your finger in some way actually *touches* the leaf. Perhaps you can visualize a beam of some sort of energy extending from the fingertip to the leaf, or perhaps you can experience the finger itself somehow transcending space to *touch* the leaf. The idea is to assume mutual influence; by your act of intention, you are to some extent influencing the leaf and the leaf is influencing you.

While your finger is *touching* the leaf, continue to be aware of your own center as the center of the universe. The leaf is also part of the universe that extends out from your center. During this exercise, due to the vector of interest expressed by your intentionality, that particular leaf is given a special significance. After approximately five minutes, let your eyes go soft and swing your hand in a small arc a few degress to either side of the leaf. Can you feel an increased sensitivity at the fingertip every time it *touches* the leaf?

Now drop your arm, shake out both hands, check your balance and center, and repeat the *touching* procedure with the same leaf. This time, if you can get a strong feeling of the leaf while moving your finger in the soft-eyed state, try the same thing with your eyes closed. If this is successful, try moving your finger even farther off the target, and check if you can find the leaf without opening your eyes.

At first, you might find it easier to establish contact with living things, but the exercise can be applied to any part of the world to which you are willing to give significance—clocks, paintings, the moon and stars. One LET student reported touching a hummingbird at a feeder, feeling the shape of its body, its pulsing throat, the vibration of its wings.

## A Synchronization Process

This process is presented as an example of large-group activity that is carried on at our classes and workshops. Suitable for groups of sixteen to one hundred or more people, this process offers the possibility of achieving the metanormal connectedness that can exist between human individuals. It requires an unobstructed indoor space large enough for free movement among all participants. As a guideline, a space that seats one hundred people will work for about forty people.

The leader begins by asking the participants to clear the floor of all extraneous objects, then to spread out and stand facing him or her so that they can turn all the way around, arms extended, without touching or just barely touching anyone else. Participants are led through the balancing and centering procedures. They are then asked to walk swiftly and at random around the room, always moving toward the empty spaces, letting those ever-changing spaces attract them. Soft eyes make it possible to do this, even at a rather fast pace, without colliding with anyone else.

When the group is thoroughly mixed, the leader asks everyone to stop, close eyes, and recheck balance and center. "Leaving your eyes closed," the leader says, "turn in place twice to the left . . . now twice to the right. . . . Let your hands float up as if in warm, salty water, then put the palms forward as if pushing a beach ball on the surface of the water. Now walk slowly, eyes closed, sensing your way through the palms of your hands, until you find a partner. Take hands with your partner, leaving eyes closed and remaining silent, and get to know her or him by what you sense through your hands."

Generally, a few people in these groups are unable to find partners with their eyes closed. The leader and assistants help them get together.

"In a moment," the leader continues, "I'm going to clap my hands. When I do, open your eyes and immediately close them again. Take a quick snapshot of your partner, in which you get only the essense of his or her face and form. Let this image, this energy essence, dissolve within you. Let it become part of you."

Two or three minutes later, the leader continues: "Now open your eyes and watch this demonstration with soft eyes." He walks around the room, stride for stride, with an assistant or one of the participants—shoulder to shoulder, arms linked. "Walk this way with your partner, assuming that the two of you are a single energy field, greater than the sum of its individual parts. Soft eyes. Keep walking until your movements are completely synchronized."

For three or four minutes, the couples walk around the room. The leader reminds them to consider themselves a single energy field. Then he asks them to gather. He passes out sheets of paper, one to each couple. The written material on all of the papers is the same excerpt from some well-written prose work. He tells them to spread out to the edges of the room and sit facing outward, each couple close together. He asks that they read aloud, synchronizing their words with their partners' words—but not with the words of the other couples. The leader suggests that the participants read not for meaning but just for rhythm, and that they assume, again, that they are one with their partners. When they come to the end of the page, they are to start over from the beginning.

Soon there is a pleasant hum throughout the room as the couples read aloud, each couple at its own speed and rhythm. During this part of the process, the breathing of most of the couples becomes synchronized.

After five minutes or so, the leader tells the couples to leave the sheets of paper where they are sitting and begin the synchronized walking again. After the walking-reading cycle is repeated, the couples are asked to sit facing each other, knees touching. Each couple then makes a single large crystalline ball between them; four hands hold and palpate the ball. The leader reminds them of the qualities of the crystalline state. He asks the participants to focus their eyes on the center of the ball, then raise it to eye level.

"Please keep your eyes focused on the center of the ball. This will mean that your partner's face will look out of focus to you. Just keep trying to hold your focus on the center of the ball. . . . Assume that this crystalline ball resonates only to one frequency. In this case, we're going to assume it's tuned to a frequency that represents a resonance common to the two of you, a key frequency in the new unified energy field. When I clap my hands, I ask that you look directly at your partner's eyes *through* the crystalline ball. Let your eyes meet through the ball, on a single, clear, resonant frequency."

The leader claps his hands, and the partners look directly into each other's eyes for two or three minutes. The leader then asks that they crush the ball out of existence between their hands, bringing their four hands together in a firm grasp, and that they rise to a standing position.

"In a moment, I'm going to ask that you silently bid your partner good-bye. Though you'll be physically separated, you'll still be joined in some significant manner. The assumption is that you'll be connected at all times with your partner for as long as this process lasts. You'll always know exactly where your partner is—without looking, without even thinking about it.

"I'm going to ask that you start the random, soft-eyed walk that you did at the beginning of this process. Then, when I clap my hands, stop, let your hands float up to the scanning position and rotate in place, scanning for your partner. Don't *look* for your partner. Keep your vision soft. Assume that you are somehow connected with your partner at all times, without thought. When you sense this connection through your hands or in any other way, zero-in and stop, facing your partner wherever he or she may be in the room."

Again, the random walk begins. When the leader feels that the group is thoroughly mixed, he claps his hand, the participants stop, rotate in place, and zero-in on their partners. This is repeated twice, still with eyes open and soft, as a practice for what is to come.

The partners are then asked to go through the same procedure with eyes barely open, so that they can see only the feet of nearby people. This, too, is repeated twice.

Finally, they are asked to walk around with eyes barely open, then, at the sound of the leader's hand clap, to close their eyes tightly and leave them closed as they zero in on their partners. Scanning for partners takes place, in this case, *with eyes completely closed*. When the partners have had a few moments to zero in, the leader asks that they open their eyes and, if necessary, correct their alignment. The closed-eye practice is repeated at least three times. The group then gathers informally for a discussion of the process.

We have found this process to give reliably good results. For example, thirty-three people participated in a Synchronization Process during our ITP class of June 25, 1993. We had the participants attempt to locate their partners with eyes closed three times. Only one person failed all three times. Four participants located their partner one of the three attempts, fourteen got direct hits two out of the three attempts, and fourteen found their partners with eyes closed all three times. We considered the possibility that some people were peeking, but close observation showed this not to be the case. Participants have often found their partners even when other people blocked their view. And there have been cases when a participant accurately pinpointed his or her partner's location even though the partner had left the room during the process without notifying anyone.

Results in exercises such as these add to a growing body of evidence that modes of sensing exist that are generally not acknowleged in our culture. We believe that our capacities in areas ranging from what we term normal to what we term metanormal are vastly greater than commonly assumed, and that by cultivating them we can enrich our lives.

# TWELVE

❉

# *The Marriage of Theory and Practice*

All those engaged in a serious calling—whether scientist or nurse, artist or contemplative—are strengthened in that calling by a sustainable philosophy that supports their work. Their practice is enhanced if they know why they must learn certain skills, why they must cultivate particular virtues, and how the elements of their practice fit together. Our classes have emphatically taught us that this holds true for integral practice. No one can endure the resistance from self and others, the doubts, the frustrations, the inevitable ups and downs of long-term discipline without a good set of reasons for doing so.

The need for a basis in theory becomes clear when the practitioners of an integral discipline have to make course corrections. The principles that guide our work have enabled us to assess the effectiveness of our programs and the progress of class members. They have helped us improve certain exercises and invent better ways to make our program effective. There is an analogy here with science in that our theory of integral transformation has been tested by the experience of class members, while, at the same time, members' experience has been guided by theory. Both our theory and our practice have developed from their mutual give-and-take.

**Some Fundamental Principles Underlying Integral Practice**

A philosophy is composed of several principles. Here are some that underlie the integral practice described in this book:

- Most of us realize just a fraction of our human potential. We live only part of the life we are given.

- The culture we inhabit reinforces only some of our latent capacities while neglecting or suppressing others. In the contemporary West, for example, there is great support for high-level athletic development but relatively little for advanced meditation and the metanormal capacities it evokes.

- Most, if not all, human attributes can give rise to extraordinary versions of themselves, either spontaneously or through transformative practice. This is the case for perception of external events, somatic awareness, communication skills, vitality, movement abilities, capacities to manipulate the environment directly, feelings of pain and pleasure, memory, cognition, volition, sense of self, love, and bodily structures.

- Extraordinary attributes, when seen as a whole, point toward a more powerful and luminous human nature, even a new type of physical embodiment in which the flesh will be suffused with new joy, beauty, and power.

- Extraordinary attributes frequently seem to be given rather than earned, and often arise fully formed from a dimension beyond ordinary functioning. Furthermore, their appearance sometimes appears to be mediated by supernormal agencies or processes (which in Jewish, Islamic, and Christian terms are called the "graces of God," in Buddhism the "workings of Buddha-nature," and in Taoism the "way of the Tao").

- A widespread realization of extraordinary attributes might lead to an epochal evolutionary turn analogous to the rise of life from inorganic matter and of humankind from its hominid ancestors.

- However, evolution meanders more than it progresses. This is an adventurous universe, in which each advance can be viewed in retrospect as a perilous journey, a close call with failure. Humankind's further advance is not guaranteed nor is the progress of any individual.

- To last, extraordinary attributes must be cultivated. For a many-sided realization of extraordinary attributes, for *integral transformation*, we need a practice that embraces body, mind, heart, and soul.

- Enduring transformative practices are comprised of several identifiable activities, or *transformative modalities*, such as disciplined self-observation, visualization of desired capacities (see chapter 7), focused surrender to emergent capacities (see chapter 5), and elicitation of the "relaxation response" (see chapter 8). Integral practices incorporate these modalities to produce a balanced development of our entire nature.

- There is an "all-at-once" quality about these transformative modalities. Like a good business deal or scientific theory, they yield great returns on investment of time and energy (see chapter 8).

- These modalities operate in everyday life to some extent, whether or not we are engaged in a formal practice. All of us, for example, are consciously guided—or unconsciously driven— by images of things we desire, and in most transformative practices such imagery is used to facilitate specific physical or psychological changes (see chapter 7). We all occasionally experience the emotional catharsis that is fundamental to many psychotherapeutic and religious disciplines, and we all sometimes practice self-observation. In other words, *all of us practice on a daily basis, albeit in a fragmented, largely unconscious manner.* Integral practice of the kind we propose in this book aims to make our fragmented practices conscious, creative, and coherent and harness them for health and growth.

- There is a powerful resonance between body, heart, mind, and soul. All levels and dimensions of human nature respond to one another, and a change in one typically facilitates a corresponding change in another, as when mental images and affirmations affect the body. This resonance exists because all manifest things arise from a common source, which is "involved" in the stuff of the universe (see below).

- To last and to be successful, integral practice must be engaged primarily for its own sake, without obsession with ends and results. Its practitioners do best when they learn to enjoy the long plateaus of the learning curve. Preoccupation with goals can cause a compulsive striving that blinds us to the emergence of unexpected goods and that inhibits the workings of grace.

- Both the theory and practice of integral transformation are still developing and require a mutual give and take. They are works in progress, requiring course corrections. Like science, they involve continual discovery.

- One reason that transformative practices require course corrections is that they can produce unbalanced development, inhibiting certain capacities while promoting others in a way that subverts lasting growth. They also can give rise to powers that serve destructive motives and therefore need to be monitored by peers and mentors.

- All human attributes depend upon one another, either directly or indirectly. For example, disciplined self-observation requires a certain measure of courage; sustained meditation requires physical stamina; the control of autonomic processes requires kinesthetic sensitivity. Integral practice addresses this aspect of human nature by embracing all aspects of body, mind, heart, and soul.

- The grace-laden nature of extraordinary attributes, and the sublimity, power, and beauty they reveal, strongly suggest that evolution on earth is an unfoldment of a prior "involution," "descent," or "implication" of that sublimity, power, and beauty in the stuff of the universe. In other words, the world's primary tendency is to manifest great goods that are hidden in it. That tendency inclines us toward extraordinary life, which can best be realized through integral practices. We develop this idea in the section that follows.

**Involution-Evolution**     Cosmologists tell us that our world began as some sort of seed, no larger perhaps than a needle point. There was a moment, they say, just the barest instant of time, when from that seed there arose enough energy to create everything in our universe. This stupendous beginning had no atoms, no elements as we know them now, and yet it contained in potentia the billions of galaxies, the millions of species on earth, the human mind and heart. From this womb of our world would come giant red stars and lovers' tears, supernovae and Bach choral masses, animal life and the ecstasy of saints. In that exploding seed was the potential for pain and glory, cruelty and redeeming grace. Our heart tells us that something more than chance was involved. A guiding spirit, an awareness, we believe was secretly there from the start.

For things could have gone wrong at many points in our world's journey. At the very beginning, in that first instant of time, if the density of the budding universe were not what it was, all of creation would have collapsed. In the words of one astrophysicist, that density required "an adjustment not of one part in a thousand, not of one in a trillion, but of one part in infinity." At one point in the evolution of the early universe, had there not been a preponderance of matter over antimatter, the first particle collisions would have yielded nothing but energy. There would have been no stars or planets, no human heart, just radiating particles for aeons to come.

Reflecting upon the stupendous cosmic coincidences and the multibillion-year defiance of odds that evolution exhibits, we sense that a purpose, a telos, calls the universe toward a greater existence. And we find such a calling in us. There is a profound affinity between the world's advance and our capacity for transformation, between the emergence of consciousness from the inorganic world and the emergence of new life in us. This affinity has led many thinkers to propose that the universe's evolution is the unfolding of a spirit, or divinity, involved in inconscient matter and energy, a divinity that presses to manifest itself more fully in the course of time. This intuition, this vision, has been developed in various ways from the beginning of the nineteenth century.

*The body is all time remembered.*

M.M.

Since about 1800, a striking number of the world's most prominent philosophers have proposed that the emergence of higher organization and higher qualities—in individuals, societies, and the world at large—is made possible by their secret existence, or immanence, in nature. The German philosopher Hegel, for example, proposed that *Geist* (the supreme Spirit) gradually reveals itself through the long dialectic of history, recovering its fundamental completeness as one aspect of itself after another is subsumed in a higher fulfillment. In *The Phenomenology of the Spirit* (1807), he traced this process through various stages of human history, from the slave of antiquity who struggled successfully against nature's difficulties to the modern intellectual's embrace of reason's highest principles, in an attempt to show how successive forms of consciousness preserve and lift up the forms that precede them.

Henry James, Sr., the father of William and Henry James, also viewed the world as an unfoldment of spirit. He was led to this view in part by the scientist-philosopher Emanuel Swedenborg. In his metaphysical treatise *Substance and Shadow* (1863), the elder James wrote: "...[A]ccording to Swedenborg, God creates us or gives us being only by thoroughly incarnating Himself in our nature; but inasmuch as this descent of the creator to creaturely limitations... involves the strictest inversion of the creative perfection...so it must necessarily provoke a corresponding ascending movement." For James, the inorganic, animal, and human realms press to manifest the divinity that is latent in them. "Whatsoever creates a thing," he wrote, "gives it being, *in*-volves the thing. The Creator involves the creature; the creature *e*-volves the Creator."

Some fifty years later, the Indian mystic and philosopher Sri Aurobindo articulated a vision of involution-evolution that resembles that of James. In his philosophical work *The Life Divine*, Aurobindo wrote:

> ...if evolution is the progressive manifestation by Nature of that which slept or worked in her, involved, it is also the overt realization of that which she secretly is. We cannot, then, bid her pause at a given stage of her evolution, nor have we the right to condemn with the religionist as perverse or with the rationalist as a disease or hallucination any intention she may evince or effort she may make to go beyond. If it be true that Spirit is involved in Matter and apparent Nature is secret God, then the manifestation of the divine in himself and the realization of God within and without are the highest and most legitimate aim possible to man upon earth.

There are significant differences between their philosophies, but both Aurobindo and James saw universal evolution arising from a previous involution of spirit in nature. James's biographer Frederic Young wrote: "To read Aurobindo's masterpiece, *The Life Divine*, is, to one who has read the senior James's works, to experience an indescribable feeling that Aurobindo and James must have corresponded and conversed with each other; so much spiritual kinship is there between the philosophies of these two thinkers!" Both the Indian and American philosophers regarded "apparent Nature" to be "secret God," and saw divinity emerging more fully through the uneven but inexorable evolution of the universe. Like other thinkers since the early nineteenth century, they "temporalized the great chain of being," to use historian Arthur Lovejoy's phrase, conceiving the world's hierarchy of inorganic, animal, and human forms "not as the inventory but as the program of nature."

Until notions of progress and the fact of evolution became prominent in the West, visions of human betterment were usually embedded in worldviews that regarded the world to be a static or cyclical existence to which time adds nothing new. In Lovejoy's words, the conception of the Chain of Being (the hierarchy of the manifest world, including matter, life, and humankind) was in accord with the Solomonic dictum that there is not—and never will be—anything new under the sun. But human visions change. Hegel, the elder James, and Aurobindo represent an historic shift of perspective by many thinkers from the view that the world is static to a belief that it is moving, however haphazardly, toward higher levels of existence. According to these philosophers, our growth as individuals is inextricably linked with the world's growth. Spirit progressively manifests through us *and* through the world's evolution. By the unfoldment of our latent capacities, we *and* the world share the ongoing manifestation of the divinity latent in nature.

For thinkers such as Hegel and Aurobindo, however, divinity also *exceeds* the manifest world. Its immanence, or "involution," does not limit its eternal and infinite existence. In this respect, such thinkers agree with mystics and philosophers East and West who did not know about evolution but who believed that the ultimate source of things was both immanent in and transcendent to the universe. In the words of the Isha Upanishad, one of India's oldest scriptures: "That moves, and That moves not. That is far, and the same is near. That is within all things, and That is outside all things." That this vision has been wedded to both evolutionary and nonevolutionary worldviews shows its lasting appeal to the philosophical imagination, and its resonance with an intuition prevalent in many times and cultures. The idea that divinity is involved in the world while at the

same time retaining its timeless and unlimited existence reflects a realization, reported by countless people since antiquity, that we enjoy
a secret alliance or identity with the founding principle of this universe. Such realization may be fleeting or lasting, spontaneous or the
product of religious practice, but it is an enduring feature of human
life. The seers of virtually every sacred tradition have expressed it
through stories, epigrams, and philosophical doctrines. For example:

- In a famous Hindu religious parable, a lost tiger cub is raised by
  sheep, perceiving itself to be one of them until another tiger
  makes it look at its reflection in a river. We typically identify
  with those around us, the parable implies, forgetting that we
  are essentially one with God.

- A well-known Zen *koan* asks: "Before your parents were born,
  what is your original face?" This line suggests that we have an
  essential subjectivity or personhood that transcends birth and
  death.

- The Platonic doctrines of *anamnesis*, or "recollection" of the
  divine ideas underlying sense impressions, is based upon the
  belief that humans have immortal souls that communed with
  those ideas before assuming a mortal body.

- Plotinus, the great mystic-philosopher of Roman antiquity,
  wrote: "God is outside of none, present unperceived to all; we
  break away from Him or rather from ourselves; what we turn
  from we cannot reach; astray ourselves, we cannot go in search
  of another; a child distraught will not recognize its father; to
  find ourselves is to know our source." The image of homecoming in this passage is expressed by the German poet Novalis in
  his famous line *immer nach hause*, "always homeward" to our
  source.

- The medieval Christian priest Meister Eckehart wrote: "The
  knower and the known are one. Simple people imagine that
  they should see God, as if He stood there and they here. This
  is not so. God and I, we are one in knowledge." And Saint
  Catherine of Genoa claimed: "My Me is God, nor do I recognize any other Me except my God Himself."

- In similar fashion, the Sufi Bayazid of Bistun exclaimed: "I went from God to God, until they cried from me in me, 'O thou I'!"

These words from Hindu, Buddhist, Platonist, Christian, and Islamic sources express the enduring realization, shared by countless people since the beginnings of recorded history, of a being ordinarily hidden but immediately recognized as our true identity (a tiger among sheep), our original face, our immortal soul, our ultimate home, our shared knowing with God, our oneness with "all the Gods." In the light of such realization, it is natural to see the world either as a stage for the individual soul's return to its source, or (as did Hegel, Aurobindo, and James) as a universal evolutionary process manifesting its secret divinity. The involution-evolution idea economically and beautifully reflects the spiritual realizations of men and women who have lived in different times and many parts of the earth. But it does more than that. This intuition, this vision, helps account for many aspects of human life, and it provides support for the principles underlying integral practice. For example:

- It gives us a theoretical basis for understanding why every human attribute can give rise to extraordinary versions of itself. If we are secretly allied with the source of the universe, we must share its all-encompassing power. We are capable of radical transformation, and can realize metanormal capacities, because that is our predisposition.

- It helps us understand our yearnings for God. If the entire universe presses to manifest its hidden divinity, then we share that impetus, which often expresses itself as a desire for the ego-surpassing love, the self-existent delight, the oneness with spirit inherent in our deepest nature.

- It helps explain humankind's inextinguishable creativity. If all the world is essentially an infinitely creative spirit, creativity must be accessible to every man, woman, and child.

- The best things in life often seem to be given rather than earned, spontaneously revealed rather than produced by deliberate effort (though practice sets the stage for most of them). This sense of grace in human affairs, which is shared by people in every land, is understandable if life's highest goods are involved in the world, waiting for the right conditions to manifest.

- At the same time, the involution-evolution idea helps us understand the transformative power of deliberate practice and the effectiveness of its essential modalities. Imagery, meditation, and focused surrender work best by aligning us with aspects of the divinity that is latent in us.

- It gives us a compelling reason for the resonance between human volition, imagery, emotion, and flesh through which psychosomatic changes appear to be mediated. If all our parts come from a common source, they must be profoundly connected. Our cells, feelings, and thoughts resonate with each other because they are parts of the same omnipresent reality. Body responds to mind, and mind to body, because they arise from the same ever-present origin.

- For all of the reasons just noted, the involution-evolution idea helps us understand the effectiveness of practices that embrace the whole person, that is, for *integral* practices. We say more about this in the section that follows.

*The universe is in the business of delivering up the unpredictable.*

G.L.

## Some Reflections on Integral Practice

A transformative practice, as we use the term in this book, is a coherent and complex set of activities that produces positive changes in an individual or group. The transformative practices that have endured longest, and that have produced the greatest changes in their practitioners, have typically embraced the whole person. The psychophysical rituals of shamanism, which open the shaman to life's multidimensional splendor; the ethical, somatic, cognitive, and spiritual family of disciplines described in Patanjali's yoga sutras; the rich ways of Zen, which have deeply influenced Japanese arts, morals, work, and play; the offering of everyday life to God in Hasidism, Sufism, and much Christian practice all embrace body, mind, heart, and soul. Each of them is an integral practice.

Such disciplines have endured for many reasons, among them these:

- They orient their practitioners toward the greater life that is latent in all our traits and virtues, all our attributes.

- They creatively use "all-at-once" responses such as the relaxation response (see chapter 8), as well as transformative modalities such as imagery and focused surrender that produce many positive outcomes at once, in a coordinated fashion.

- They help prevent the negative activities caused by parts of one's nature that more limited practices leave neglected (see chapters 13 and 14).

All human virtues and attributes, and all transformative methods, depend to some extent on one another. To develop awareness, for example, we need a certain measure of courage; to achieve strong control of autonomic processes, we need a yielding sensitivity to our body; to develop a powerful will, we must sometimes adapt to particular circumstances. Furthermore, the cultivation of one attribute often benefits others. Spiritual illuminations sometimes happen in sports, for example, even to athletes who don't seek or expect them; while conversely, some contemplatives exhibit amazing physical abilities in conjunction with mystical experiences. Such capacities and experiences emerge in clusters because all our attributes, whether ordinary or extraordinary, are intertwined with one another.

No virtue, no attribute, no transformative method stands alone. That is the case even though (1) extraordinary capacities can exist side by side with psychological and physical deficiencies; (2) different physiological systems, though interdependent, operate with considerable autonomy; and (3) much human activity is affected by dissociated volitions, attitudes, memories, and emotions. Though all our parts have a certain degree of independence, they affect one another directly or indirectly. That is why enduring transformative practices address the whole person.

We cannot escape our many-sidedness. One way or another, each dimension of our complex nature lays claim to its fulfillment. By honoring the diverse claims within us, many-sided disciplines have proved their worth through the long course of human history. Today, we have the opportunity to develop such disciplines by incorporating insights and methods from all the sacred traditions, from modern psychology and medical science, and from other fields. Elaborating this thought in *The Future of the Body*, Michael Murphy wrote:

"Among the advantages we enjoy today in creating integral practices is the proliferation of disciplines for cognitive, emotional, and bodily development. General semantics, linguistics, and related disciplines, most of them influenced directly or indirectly by the analytic philosophy that has flourished in British and American universities, give us new understanding of mental process. Never before have the foibles of thought, the good and bad habits of mind, the means of clear intellectual activity, been so thoroughly examined. . . . transformative practice needs the lessons such disciplines offer. The education of emotions, too, has developed in recent times. Modern depth psychology has increased our understanding of repressed or dissociated feelings, unconscious motivations, and psychodynamics in general, while offering new approaches to health and exceptional functioning. By their insights into the effects of unconscious volitions, and by their discoveries about culture's formative influence on each person's makeup, the human sciences complement the transpersonal perspectives embedded in the religious traditions. Since Freud, the modern West has produced a yoga of the emotions that can support other transformative disciplines. Contemporary psychotherapy, and the affective education it informs, give us many ways to cultivate our relationships, volitions, and feelings to enhance integral practices.

"At the same time, medical science, contemporary sports, and somatic education give us the basis for a physical training with unprecedented variety, richness, and robustness. Never before have so many athletic abilities been cultivated, nor have so many people tried to stretch their physical limits in so many ways, nor has human physiology been so thoroughly understood. Modern sports and the attendant fields of sports medicine and sports psychology constitute a vast laboratory for bodily transformation. Discoveries by athletes and their trainers of optimal methods for superior performance; the growing lore among somatic educators about sensory, kinesthetic, and motor skills training; and the developing insights about bodily functioning provided by medical science can assist any practice oriented toward metanormal embodiment. The cognitive, affective, and physical aspects of human functioning, in short, can be improved by numerous discoveries that few, if any previous cultures enjoyed. These discoveries and the transformative disciplines they inform could comprise a yoga of yogas, as it were, to embrace our many capacities."

*Both spontaneously and through transformative practice, a new evolutionary domain is rising in the human species.*

M.M.

### Readings that Can Enhance Your Practice

During our ITP courses, class members explored these and other ideas supporting integral practice. They did this mainly through reading assignments, regularly scheduled seminars, and informal discussions. This exploration was a shared undertaking, in which leaders and participants alike developed their understanding of the theories and disciplines involved. We (Leonard and Murphy) deepened our appreciation of certain previously held principles. For example, we were confirmed in our sense that the appearance of metanormal capacities is hard to predict and that their development requires a surrender to processes beyond normal consciousness. But we were also surprised by some of the things we learned. We were sobered, for example, by the extent to which transformative practice can alter *every* part of our lives. Integral practice, we found, can be more integral than one first imagines. It can challenge intimate relationships, vocational commitments, and our most fundamental patterns of thought, emotion, and bodily functioning. While most of our guiding principles have stood through numerous tests, giving us an anchor for practice, some have been refined or discarded.

So how can the reader make a marriage of theory and integral practice? How do you establish a cognitive track within your own discipline? Here are some first suggestions.

Establish a reading list, starting with Michael Murphy's *The Future of the Body* and George Leonard's *Mastery*, which together with this book present an overview of ideas and practices related to integral transformation. If the *Future of the Body* is too long for you, read Parts One and Three, using Part Two and the appendices for further reading. *Mastery* is shorter and elaborates several principles and observations that are presented here. These two books will give you both practical suggestions about integral discipline and a general theory of human transformation. We also recommend the books listed in Appendix C.

All of these books and articles can contribute to your thinking about integral transformation. None of them, however, has the final word about the subjects they address. Each represents just part of the world's work-in-progress to understand God, humanity, and our evolving universe. Nevertheless, any one of the readings listed in Appendix C can lead you to further information and to ideas that illumine the life we are given. Most of them cite material you can explore, and several have useful bibliographies. Through reading and group discussions, you can begin with one or more of them and fan out to others. Such inquiry leads to new fields of knowledge, and will almost certainly open up new kinds of experience. Our ITP classes have shown us that intellectual activity is a doorway to more than the intellect itself.

For example, we read that meditation can reveal a being that underlies ordinary feeling and thought and that connects us profoundly with others. From then on—as if by magic—such being arises spontaneously, in meetings with friends or talking to someone we deeply love or sitting alone at a restaurant table. An innocent-seeming sentence, just eight or ten simple words, can have tremendous effects upon us. A description of a particular ability, even a mere name for it, can evoke that ability or help us realize that we already have it to some degree. Look for such recognitions in your reading and group discussions. Discovery will lead to further discovery.

Ideas have the power to open us up. They also help us integrate capacities that initially seem strange or threatening. We read, for example, about meditation states in which one experiences "stereophonic" hearing. Learning that some contemplatives cultivate this auditory capacity, we are emboldened to explore it ourselves. Think of some ability that once disturbed you. What led you to value it? What was told to you, or what did you read, that helped you see that it was good? Integral practices sometimes produce potentially creative experiences that at first are disturbing, and for that reason require a mind-set that is favorable to them. Reading books about extraordinary experiences such as those listed in Appendix C, along with group discussions of them, can help you develop that mind-set. Our conceptual picture of human possibility develops in concord with all our parts. As our *vision* of integral transformation grows, we recognize, and therefore can cultivate, more and more latent capacities. Building a philosophy that embraces an ever wider range of human possibilities will broaden your practice as it broadens your intellect.

As we have pointed out, there is an "all-at-once" quality about certain activities that constitute transformative practice. Like a good business investment or scientific theory, such activities yield strong returns on investment. We repeat that observation here because the cognitive aspects of integral practice have this all-at-once character. A good intellectual grasp of our ITP programs went along with improvements in the emotional and physical functioning of class members. The ancient adage that body, mind, heart, and soul mirror one another has been confirmed by our ITP experience. By embracing the intellect, integral practice enhances *all* our parts.

# THIRTEEN

# The Magic of Community

In the beginning there was community. When our species, *Homo sapiens*, first emerged in Africa some 150,000 years ago or more, we lived in small, close-knit hunting and gathering bands. It was to this way of life, not farming or urban living, that our bodies evolved. Our bones, musculature, central and peripheral nervous systems, endocrine systems, immune systems, and brains are not significantly different from those of our Stone Age ancestors. To these people, existence without community was unthinkable, impossible. Banishment meant death.

How can we summon up the *feeling* of community, of oneness with others that made our life? Ancient stones offer testimony on campsites, tools, successful hunts, episodes of violent death. Surviving hunting and gathering bands give clues to a way of living that takes us back to our earliest days. And even now there are moments around the campfire beneath the stars with good friends and good food and drink when that vanished life reappears, immediate in our own consciousness, a life full of talk and laughter, rich in ritual and ceremony, a life of langorous nights and leisurely days interspersed with periods of intense physical challenge and moments of risk and high adventure. As our knowledge of the distant past deepens, we realize that it was not only building or working that shaped our bodies and brains, for our primitive ancestors had no permanent dwelling places, no jobs. We were also born to art, to music and dance, to a vital feeling for what we now inadequately term the spiritual realm, a consciousness of the variety, immediacy, and beauty of the unseen. Permeating all this was the intricate web of relationships that held us close in the love and nurturance of those we walked with, ate with, slept with. To say "human being" is to invoke community.

*An education devoid of the ecstatic moment is the mere shadow of education.*

G.L.

With the development of agriculture, the social unit expanded from the small hunting and gathering band to the tribe, the chiefdomship, the city-state, the nation-state; from a group of thirty or so men, women, and chidlren to groups of hundreds, thousands, millions. To these larger groups we gave allegiance and derived a sense of identity and belonging. But still there was our primal, biological need for smaller communities made up of people we could know and touch. This need was fulfilled through clubs organized around work, play, and politics, through clans, secret societies, church groups, the neighborhood, the extended family.

In today's rootless, restless, fragmented society, the bonds of community are badly frayed and sometimes ripped apart. Young people's innate need for community expresses itself through loyalty to street gangs. Adults who have moved far from their families and don't know their neighbors adopt a media community. With no Mrs. Green down the street to relate with or gossip about, many of us follow the intimate doings of various celebrities. Print tabloids spawn tabloid TV. But this one-way relationship with a shadow play of celebrities is intrinsically unsatisfying. Too often in our lives today, real community is lacking, a need unfulfilled.

The destructive effects of this isolation along with the healing and transformative powers of community has begun to show up in scientific studies. In his pioneering program of heart disease reversal without drugs or surgery, Dean Ornish worked with the premise that isolation is a major factor in sickness and that the support groups in his program are a major factor in the transformations of coronary arteries (see chapter 2). Another researcher, David Spiegel of Stanford University, conducted a study of eighty-six women with metastatic breast cancer. The study was designed to test the alleviation of pain. Fifty of the women—the treatment group—were randomly assigned to meet in support groups for an hour once a week. A control group of thirty-six women did not meet in support groups. All the women in the study received standard medical treatment.

After a year, the women in the treatment group showed a significant alleviation of their pain.

Then came a surprise. Four years after the study began, all the women in the control group had died from this devastating disease while one-third of the women in the treatment group were still alive. As it turned out, the women in the treatment group lived an average of eighteen months longer than those in the control group—the only difference between the two groups being the creation of a community that met *only one hour once a week*. Other recent studies show similar results.

The longing for community is universal. A 1993 Lou Harris and Associates survey asked a national sample of people what was the most important thing in their life. More than half (56 percent) of those interviewed said that relationships with friends and family were the most important. This was followed by religious faith (21 percent), doing something to make the world a better place (12 percent), career fulfillment (5 percent), and monetary success (5 percent).

Our own Integral Transformative Practice class offered us the opportunity to witness the singular power of community. Cycle 93 participants were asked to rate twelve aspects of the program in terms of their importance in enhancing their practice. "ITP community" ranked third, just behind "Affirmations" and "Kata," just in front of "LET Exercises." For many of the participants, the community had even greater importance. Most of them adjourned to a nearby cafe for socializing on a regular basis following the Saturday classes. On their own, they organized evening meetings at members' homes to meditate, practice the Kata, discuss readings, or just get together. After we stopped leading classes in order to concentrate on evaluating our results and writing this book, a group of participants continued the program on their own, holding a full schedule of classes and off-site meetings.

There is something magical about any intense, tightly knit group of people working together and playing together, a feeling of being in the world while at the same time being apart from it, *apart together*. We believe that even those of us who have not experienced that magic hear its distant music, feel its ancient call. A transformative community is a nearly indispensible launching pad for transformation. Such a community can create the context and the confidence for a transforming journey.

**How Culture Shapes
the Body and Being**

In recent decades, anthropologists have shown that many human attributes, which biologists used to think were inherited, are in fact culturally conditioned. Smiling, frowning, and other facial expressions have been proven to differ fundamentally from culture to culture. Sociologist David Efron found that assimilated Jews and Italians in New York City gesture differently than do their unassimilated counterparts. In a worldwide survey of postural habits, Gordon Hewes showed that we sit, kneel, stand, and recline in ways that are socially determined. It's now clearly established that human posture, physique, motor habits, and body image, as well as emotions and thought patterns, are culturally shaped. Think for a moment about the manner in which your body and mind have been influenced by others. Where did your habitual gestures come from? Whose laughter does yours resemble? Consider your food preferences, your style of dress, the kinds of exercise you like. Chances are that you can identify a particular person or group that led you to them.

Even our spiritual experiences are shaped by culture. Religious scholar Steven Katz edited a collection of essays, *Mysticism and Philosophical Analysis*, which presses home the fact that different traditions give rise to different kinds of contemplative realization. None of our experiences are immune to social influence. The most independent people are shaped by their acquaintances, friends, family, and by the institutions to which they belong.

We emphasize this observation because the cultures we inhabit either help or hinder the development of particular attributes. Generally speaking, *human capacities develop most fully in cultures that prize them*. Because Renaissance Florence celebrated art, it produced some of history's greatest artists. Because Americans love sports, America produces great athletes. Appreciating this fact of human life, educators and religious teachers have built institutions specifically designed to support the attributes they deemed to be important. Saint Paul and Saint Peter formed communities to nurture Christian virtues. To foster the experiences they valued, the Buddha founded a *sangha* (fellowship), Plato the Academy, Aristotle the Lyceum, Saint Benedict his monastery. The university was developed in the late Middle Ages to support the kinds of learning the Church generally shunned. Today, we need to develop social structures to nurture integral practice. That is what we had in mind when we started our ITP classes.

Think of your own attempts to cultivate new capacities. Have you been frustrated by lack of support? How many times have your programs for growth failed because you didn't have friends or mentors to help you? Contemporary society encourages us in countless ways toward a life of distraction. Advertisers invite us to consume things we don't need—or even want—through television, magazines, and uninvited mailings. With the proliferation of telephones, much leisure time is filled with unsolicited conversation. To establish disciplines of any type, we have to counteract many distractions of modern life, and this is particularly true if we undertake long-term transformative practices. For the kinds of growth described in this book, we need healthy group support. Here are some ways to establish communities for integral practice.

## The Transforming Alchemy of Listening

First, a support group can consist of two people. Our own experience has taught us that one partner can decisively improve your practice. A single ally can bring new perspectives to your difficulties, give helpful counsel, and lift your spirits through sympathetic listening. He or she can challenge you when inertia holds you back and provide encouragement when the going is tough. Sharing the ups and downs of long-term practice can produce a lasting solidarity. Lasting friendship is perhaps the greatest blessing that such discipline brings us. Those of us who have joined with colleagues in a significant work appreciate the depth of enjoyment this sort of collaboration brings. It is one of life's greatest pleasures.

We suggest that you find a friend who shares your commitment to integral practice. Set regular meeting times with her or him to explore the problems you're having. Schedule periods for meditation, physical exercise, affirmations, and philosophical inquiry. Check each other's progress. Provide challenge and needed support. As time goes on, you'll both learn from and teach one another.

But the sharing of practice, of course, needn't be limited to a single friend. Winning sports teams, excited classrooms, creative religious communities, and other kinds of inspired groups have fostered accomplishments ranging from the healing of chronic afflictions to historic advances in science and religious understanding. Many are the cohorts that have facilitated extraordinary functioning. Roger Bannister, for example, broke the four-minute barrier in the mile, a feat once thought impossible, through his concerted effort with two running partners, Chris Chataway and Chris Brasher. The three men trained together for many months, and carefully planned their racing strategies. During their historic race, which took place in Britain during 1954, Brasher paced the first two laps and Chataway the third, putting Bannister in a position from which he sprinted to his record-setting time of 3:59:4. "We had done it—the three of us!" Bannister wrote. "We shared a place where no man had ventured—secure for all time, however fast men might run miles in the future. We had done it where we wanted, when we wanted, how we wanted!" Scientific advances, too, are frequently made by mutually supportive groups. In *The Double Helix*, James Watson chronicled his discovery with Francis Crick of DNA. Reading the book, one senses the mutual stimulation the two biologists experienced as they made their historic breakthrough.

To foster integral practice, you can create a group that provides the stimulation that highly motivated athletic and scientific teams enjoy. At our Saturday meetings and at the midweek meetings arranged by teachers and participants, there was typically a marked excitement and sense of homecoming. Both ITP cycles produced a self-generating sense of momentum. You can form a similar group and create the same kind of excitement.

Begin by setting regular meeting times, including sessions to meditate, share matters of the heart, study philosophy, and do physical exercise. It's important, we believe, that you include activities that nurture body, mind, heart, and soul. Play is important. Lend imagination to your strength and aerobic work, to your mutual counseling, to your intellectual exchanges. Join spontaneity and steadfastness.

To nurture self-awareness and general psychological health, participants can begin by sharing their concerns with fellow participants. Trust has to be built for intimate sharing, and nothing builds it faster than a sympathetic ear. That is the case because we are likely to feel invalidated if, upon revealing something that's troubling us, we get immediate reassurance or advice. So deeply ingrained are these modes of response that even the psychologically sophisticated in our groups sometime had to be reminded not to leap in to reassure or analyze or fix things. In group support sessions, we urged our participants to reveal themselves through feelings rather than opinions or judgments. And we urged those listening to be fully present, willing to hear the speaker out. Reassurances or advice might be given later—best of all when asked for.

Empathic listening builds a climate that helps group members reveal themselves. Through self-revelation in an atmosphere of trust, we learn to accept attributes we had not recognized or fully appreciated. We get new perspectives on our habitual patterns of feeling and thought and new foundations for work on ourselves. Through the growing self-acceptance that is encouraged by the presence of empathic listeners, our wounds can be healed and our capacities developed more freely. Many of the more extraordinary human capacities wither away simply through the self-censorship that springs from fear of ridicule—or worse.

That this fear is not without foundation is illustrated by the story of a woman (not a member of the ITP group) who had a powerful mystical experience while doing houshold chores. It was a beautiful day. Gazing out of a window at trees and birds and sky while washing dishes, she fell into a contemplative mood. Suddenly she was struck by the powerful certainty that, in essence, we are all one. This certainty—one that holds an honored place in the most revered spiritual traditions—filled her with a happiness she had never known, and she hurried to tell her husband what she was experiencing. Far from sharing her joy, he became deeply disturbed. After a couple of days during which she maintained her faith in the validity of her experience, he insisted she see a psychiatrist. At this point, realizing that what she had experienced had no safe place in the culture in which she lived, she told the psychiatrist that she guessed we weren't all one after all. She returned to her workaday life, exorcised of the extraordinary, cured of her joy, and filled with a lingering sadness over a new certainty: that she would never let herself have such an experience again.

What happened to this woman was extreme, but the self-censorship of experiences such as hers is extremely common. Even in our ITP group, among people who were dedicating themselves to the realization of human potential, we found it difficult at first to elicit verbal expression of their extraordinary experiences. It took time to develop the trust that would allow material on the fringes of consciousness and beyond the bounds of cultural consensus to be given voice. And it took the presence of empathic listeners:

*We can conceive of a future without high-rises. But a humanity without music and love is not just inconceivable; it is impossible.*

G.L.

- listeners who are interested and who really care about others,

- listeners who are willing to forego ego and the need to spout opinions,

- listeners who seek neither to add to nor to take away from what is being said,

- listeners who are patient and willing to withhold judgment for a while,

- listeners who can say, "Yes, I really hear you"—and mean it.

There is a transforming alchemy in such listening.

As intimacy and mutual acceptance in your group increase, participants are more and more likely to enjoy the give and take of ideas as well as experiences. Intellectual embarrassments will fade and curiosity will develop. New ideas arise from integral practice and can be tested in group discussions. Encourage inquiry. Encourage debate. Listen! Excitement about the vision of integral transformation will grow and can be fed by readings such as those proposed in Appendix C.

## The Dangers of Charisma

But a warning. Though we need communities to support practice, such communities can become destructive. They can diminish as well as facilitate their participants' autonomy, growth, and fulfillment. For example, many groups that are dedicated to personal growth are founded or taken over by a dominant individual who undermines the well-being of its members. Think of Jonestown or the Branch Davidians of Waco, Texas. Jim Jones and David Koresh, the leaders of those communities, did not have peers who could check their destructive influence. Exalted rhetoric, charisma, even spiritual gifts by themselves do not guarantee a leader's goodness. There is reason to be suspicious of gurus who take charge of a person's entire life. In our ITP classes, the four leaders gave one another helpful criticism. *And we listened carefully to feedback from group participants.* To deal with the complexities of integral practice, we need multiple mentors. No one today, we believe, can guide someone in all dimensions of human growth.

But even leaderless communities can hinder their members' development. Contemplative retreats, for example, sometimes attract people who don't relate happily to others and reinforce members' isolation by divorcing them from creative human contact. Therapeutically oriented groups sometimes rationalize self-indulgence as psychic liberation or promote excessive confrontation among its participants in the name of openness and honesty. Practice groups of many persuasions stifle intellectual growth by punishing divergent thought.

When communities celebrate some virtues at the expense of others, or when they support narrow beliefs, they limit possibilities for growth. And when they are strengthened in such activities by genuine advances they facilitate among their members, they can become powerful obstacles to integral transformation. While producing a few good outcomes, some practice groups stand in the way of their members' well-rounded development.

Most of us need communities to nurture transformative practice, but we have to make sure they genuinely serve us. While accepting the support and challenges they give us, we need not be limited by them. The final authority in any transformative practice is the individual practitioner.

## The Transformative Power of Love

Early in the twentieth century, Sigmund Freud conceived his principle of Eros, a tendency of all things animal and vegetable to join in larger entities, so that life might be prolonged and brought into higher development. At the beginning of time, in a universe made only of hydrogen and helium and intense energy, there was nothing we would call "life." Yet something akin to Freud's erotic principle, some inexorable tendency toward joining, toward the creation of form and complexity, seemed to have been operating.

The universe also involves destruction and dissolution—what Freud called Thanatos—and repulsion as well as attraction. But within the galaxies attraction predominates. The electron, it seems, "wants" to mate with the proton. The hydrogen atom "wants" to join the oxygen atom. The strong nuclear force binds the nucleus in exquisite strength and closeness. And gravity, the weakest of the four major forces in the universe, is entirely attraction, holding all others in its enormous embrace.

*Love something and watch it blossom.*

M.M.

In the face of its long history of meandering, of extinctions and close calls, the stuff of the universe reveals its desire to join, to make more complex, highly ordered entities. The poet Dante said it another way: "Love is what moves the sun and the stars." We believe that a community is nothing if it doesn't foster love, an unconditional love that accepts us for what we are while moving us toward the higher good. Pronouncements, books, and statistics pale beside its transformative power.

## Changing the World by Changing Your Own Heart

We have suggested that cosmic evolution as we know it, from the big bang to the present moment, is finally an expression of Eros, of love. If this is so, how then can we doubt that love stands as the highest and most fundamental human impulse? In integral practice, we feel that love can be expressed in service to others, not just to friends and family and fellow practitioners but also to those in the larger community. We understand that there are many practical reasons for this expression. To serve others accrues to benign self-interest. It exalts us in the world's eyes. It produces positive publicity for our commercial enterprises. It makes us feel good. Those who serve others in love and kindness enjoy better health and live longer.

All this is well and good and not to be denigrated or dismissed. But we believe that there is an even higher possibility in aspiring to serve others in love and kindness, not even for the sake of transformation, but simply because that is a true expression of who we are, a fundamental condition of the path upon which we walk. Love doesn't have to wait for its recipients to be worthy of it. We can love others as they are. The world doesn't have to justify itself for us. We can love the world as it is. "If I love the world as it is," writes the novelist Petru Dumitriu, "I am already changing it: a first fragment of the world has been changed, and that is my own heart."

Perhaps all transformation begins with such a change of heart.

# FOURTEEN

# The Ultimate Adventure

The program we have described in this book has proved to be of significant value to most of those who have participated in it, with extraordinary outcomes for some. There's no doubt in our minds that a regular, long-term practice that involves body, mind, heart, and soul, and that aims at good health and the cultivation of our untapped potenials, can enhance individual lives and contribute to the social good.

In the transformations that emerge from an integral practice, the matter of social support is particularly important. It is difficult even to discuss such transformations if everyone around us stands ready to prejudge and invalidate. On the other hand, there is the danger of cultic pressure to see things that don't exist. The nonauthoritarian program we have championed in these pages, along with objective reality checks wherever possible, can help us safely past this pitfall. We feel that as the number of people engaged in the quest for transformation increases, the number of successes will increase even faster. If a significant minority of a society's people consciously and constructively engage in such a quest, we could see something new on this planet: one of those events that cannot be adequately predicted by what has gone before.

## Dangers and Difficulties on the Path

But make no mistake. Transformation is not automatic nor is it "easy." In several preceding chapters, we've described problems that arise during integral practice. We have said, for example, that affirmations must be chosen with care and creatively refined or abandoned in the light of unfolding experience. We've noted certain dangers of physical exercise and have urged patient sensitivity to the body's messages during aerobic sports, strength training, and performance of the ITP Kata. We've counseled avoidance of dietary extremes. We've reviewed certain ways in which groups hinder as well as further our development. And we've emphasized the resistance to change, the necessary homeostasis that all of us encounter during any long-term effort to change. To repeat: there can be difficulty in virtually any aspect of transformative discipline.

But the degree of such difficulty varies from person to person. Some people find immediate pleasure in physical training, while others do not. Some easily adopt a healthful diet, while others feel deprived. The joys of meditation come naturally to certain people but not to everyone. As you take up an integral practice, it is useful to remember that some parts of it will come easily, but that some might not. And beyond that, the path of transformation might entail pain you don't want or expect.

## Pitfalls and Promises

Any significant shift in consciousness, in how we perceive the world, can be disorienting. Sometimes, simply by relaxing their shoulders during the balancing and centering exercise described in chapter 6, people who have been almost entirely out of touch with their bodies will become aware of bodily sensations they haven't felt since childhood. Even something as gentle and benign as this can cause temporary dizziness or trembling. And powerful experiences of union with the divine or of the oneness of existence can prove much more troubling. This is especially true of people who are not firmly grounded in their bodies or of people with a history of mental illness.

But there is an opposite danger. Transformative practice can reinforce limiting traits and thus hinder integral development. Rather than sweeping us beyond ourselves, it can help solidify our limitations. For example, meditation can—by its very success—lead people who have difficulty relating with others into social withdrawal. Contemplative bliss can provide a defense against the challenges of personal relationship and the adventures of the greater world.

Physical regimens, too, can be obstacles to growth. Some people become obsessively self-centered through running, weight lifting, or other body-enhancing regimens. The world today is filled with fit, well-toned people who have constricted emotional, intellectual, and spiritual lives. Psychological work can also be limiting when, for example, it rationalizes impulse-ridden behavior as the release of repressed emotion or an expression of authenticity, or when it fosters one trait (such as honest self-expression) at the expense of others (such as empathy and kindness).

Transformative practice can also reinforce limiting beliefs. Most of us know someone who, in the passion of his or her recent spiritual experience, has become fanatical about a particular guru, teaching, or cult. Countless people have tightened their lives around a limited set of ideas or a dogmatic teacher. But a passionate life doesn't have to be narrowed in this way. Our practice can be deep while our personal autonomy grows. We can be faithful to our path while pursuing intellectual discovery.

And a practice can subvert many-sided development by emphasizing certain virtues over others. Every culture, organization, and family does this. Think of your own upbringing, your workplace, your community. In these millieus, which virtues have taken precedence? Honesty over kindness? Courage over love? Or vice versa? Have you been shaped by these preferences? In our view, integral practice requires a recognition that all virtues, like all aspects of practice and human growth, are largely interdependent. It's difficult, if not impossible, to cultivate deep feeling for others without both sensitivity and the courage to face pain, without both strength and tenderness. It's hard to meditate for long without both tenacity and yielding, one-pointedness and the capacity for surrender. For integral practice, many virtues are needed.

You can even limit yourself to some degree by realizing authentic, but partial, kinds of extraordinary functioning. Particular traits, beliefs, and virtues can be given too much prominence, or even destructive sway in one's life by a genuine, but partial, experience of the transcendent. Some people, for example, have been led by a powerful mystical experience to perceive ordinary life as ugly, meaningless, or empty, and have thus been stimulated to believe that the world is incapable of significant transformation. Their genuine spiritual realization lends credence to a limited belief about human possibility and supports their cultivation of just some of the traits and virtues required for integral development. To come full circle on this, we can even imagine the idea of the integral, of fully balanced practice, becoming rigid and dogmatic. There are obviously geniuses of the mind who, without fully developing the body, have made great contributions. The same is true in other aspects of our being. And there are obviously times in the lives of all of us when we have stressed one part of our development at the expense of others for a good cause with good results. We strongly believe in the ancient celebration of the whole person and feel that integral practice generally provides the smoothest journey on the path of transformation. But we feel it's even more important to allow for benign human eccentricity and to avoid dogma, whatever form it takes.

Metanormal experience can produce ego inflation. Every sacred tradition warns against grandiosity following illumination. Among the safeguards against such inflation are the monitoring of practioners by mentors and friends; the monitoring of mentors by fellow mentors and the community of practice; the celebration of humor in transformative practice; the cultivation of self-understanding; and reminders about the dangers of spiritual grandiosity drawn from religion and modern psychology. Contact with ego-surpassing powers isn't all goodness and light. If we are not balanced and centered, it can cause mental and emotional instability. If we lack healthy relationships, it can foster excessive withdrawal from others. If it fires our passion for perfection, it can contribute to unhealthy obsessions with diet, physical exercise, and cleanliness.

Such difficulties are sometimes loosely characterized as features or products of the human "shadow." This term, as it is commonly used today, was made famous by the psychiatrist Carl Jung and refers in a catch-all way to the unexamined darkness of human nature. The shadow harbors great energies and impulses that can express themselves in negative ways but also, if acknowledged and integrated, can serve as rich sources of creative power. We conclude this chapter by invoking the metaphor the shadow contains. There are dark places to cross in the journey of transformation, but they might contain priceless treasures. When you come to them, stay centered, stay aware, stay in touch with those who support you. Above all, stay on the path.

## A Renewed Sense of Aliveness, A Love that Asks Nothing in Return

Throughout our practice, we have taken care to remind ourselves of the stupendous miracle of existence, the ultimate value of every life. We have celebrated our connectedness with all living things and with the stuff of the inorganic world. We have viewed every step in the cosmic journey, from the birth of the universe to the ever-flowing present moment, as our genealogy, and have experienced ourselves as a part of, not apart from, all that we behold or ever could behold. Many who have practiced with us have found the aliveness that has come from our practice to be transformative in and of itself.

*Life has one ultimate message: "Yes!" repeated in infinite number and variety.*

G.L.

To awaken can be painful, for it opens us to a poignant awareness of the pervasive waste of life around us and in us. But the eventual rewards are great. We no longer need horrors to jolt us awake. To see a sunrise is enough. To look into a friend's or lover's eyes, to truly *see* another human being, is enough. To hear a distant strain of music, or a child's laughter, is enough. With this awakening, this renewed aliveness, there generally comes a love for others, a love that asks nothing in return. Such love doesn't imply the denial of evil; the world is a dangerous place and awakening also means being aware of those dangers and standing ready to take centered action to confront wrong when necessary. But the ego-transcending love remains, and it spreads in concentric circles like ripples on a pond, kindling similar feelings in more of those it touches than we might imagine.

There are many powerful forces in the world, and some of them—cynicism, greed, ethnic hatred, heedless ambition, armies, and huge, impersonal organizations, to name a few—have a particular power to destroy. But a love that asks nothing in return is perhaps even more powerful, for it seeks to create, not destroy. Only a long series of close calls has given us this life. Again and again, over aeons of time, often against long odds, Eros has finally won the day. Are we willing to consider the possibility of a society in which love prevails?

### THE DIVINE POTENTIAL OF THE SPECIES

We believe that by the very nature of things, each of us carries a spark of divinity in every cell and that we have the potential to manifest powers of body, mind, heart, and soul beyond our present ability to imagine. We believe that a society could find no better primary intention, no more appropriate compass course for its programs and policies, than the realization of every citizen's positive potential. We mean the potential inherent in every aspect of our lives, from the most commonplace to the most extraordinary, the hidden capabilities that wait to be summoned forth, not just in the mind but also in the body, heart, and soul. Such a compass course might create clarity where there is now confusion and bring the human psyche into harmony with nature and the cosmos. At best, it could open the way to the ultimate adventure, during which much of what has been metanormal would become normal, and some who read these pages would be privileged to share the next stage in the world's unfolding splendor.

# *Further Resources for Practice*

Since this book was first published, we've produced a DVD called *The Tao of Practice: Exercises and Imaging for the Body, Mind, Heart, and Soul.* The series of exercises on this DVD is designed as a daily, forty-minute practice for people with busy lives. George Leonard offers detailed instruction on certain sections of the ITP Kata, then leads the viewer through a full session of the ITP Kata. The DVD is priced at $19.95.

In addition, we are exploring the possibility of furthering the work described in this book through a Center for Transformative Practice. The kind of center we are considering might bear a superficial resemblance to a health club, in that it would be open from early morning to evening, seven days a week. It would have a staff of carefully chosen teachers, and would be available to people of all ages, with daily classes in meditation, mental imagery, volitional training, physical movement, strength and aerobic exercise, interpersonal relations, and other transformative disciplines.

Such a facility might also present seminars and lectures on topics related to personal and social transformation. Participants could choose from any of a number of programs, enjoying the option of designing their own practice, emphasizing the kinds of change they might desire. There could be special tracks for those who would like to make commitments and affirmations toward personal transformation. Intensive short-term programs could be offered to people from out of town who wish to spend a week or two developing a personal ITP program they can take home with them. Ideally, a center of this sort would promote the simultaneous pursuit of theory, practice, and research related to the development of the whole person. It would constitute a new kind of social institution, a learning organization for the body, mind, heart, and soul, designed for long-term transformation without cult or dogma.

For information on *The Tao of Practice* videotape or on our plans for fostering the practice of ITP throughout the world, visit our Web site at www.ITP-Life.com or write to ITP, P.O. Box 609, Mill Valley, CA 94942.

APPENDIX   B

# *Statistical Summary: Cycle 93*

Two questionnaires were filled out by participants during the 1993 Cycle. Results from the final questionnaire (November 20, 1993) were used for statistical anlaysis. Thirty participants finished the 1993 Cycle and completed the questionnaire.

The mean scores for progress made toward realizing affirmations, on a scale of from 0 to 10, are presented here, as compared with scores from the 1992 Cycle (standard deviations in parentheses):

|  | Cycle 92 | Cycle 93 |
|---|---|---|
| Affirmation 1 | 5.67 (3.00) | 6.30 (3.16) |
| Affirmation 2[1] | 4.30 (3.06) | -12.60% (11.28) |
| Affirmation 3 | 4.53 (2.76) | 6.67 (3.20) |
| Affirmation 4 | 6.58 (2.32) | 8.30 (1.26) |
| Average of affirmations | 5.30 (1.53) (av. of all 4) | 7.09 (1.65) (av. of 1, 3, and 4) |

1 The scores for Affirmation 2 are not comparable. In 1992, Affirmation 2 was "exceptional" on a scale of 0 to 10. In 1993, it was percent change in body fat.

**Selected items from the questionnaire of November 20, 1993, followed by mean scores (underlined) and standard deviations (italicized)**

On average, how many times a week have you done the Kata since learning it? 3.95 *1.21*

How vivid and well focused is your induction and imaging during the Kata, on a scale of 0 to 10, with 0 being not vivid and focused at all and 10 being extremely vivid and completely focused? 6.50 *2.30*

On the average, how many minutes of aerobic exercise have you done per week since beginning this program? 243.53 minutes *121.37*

On the average, how many times a week have you done strength training over the last six months? 2.46 *1.83*

Over the last seven days, how conscious have you been of what you have eaten, on a scale of 0 to 10, with 0 being totally unconscious and 10 being totally conscious? 8.83 *1.51*

On a scale of 0 to 10, how would you rate the healthfulness of the diet you have followed over the last six months, especially in terms of avoiding a high fat content? 7.10 *2.63*

On a scale of 0 to 10, how well do you understand the theory behind Integral Transformative Practice and bodily transformation? 8.23 *1.74*

On a scale of 0 to 10, how faithfully have you completed your reading assignments? 6.73 *2.18*

On a scale of 0 to 10, how promptly and fully have you stayed current with teachers and fellow participants in letting them know any significant feelings and considerations that would affect your participation in the class? 8.17 *1.62*

On a scale of 0 to 10, how well satisfied are you with your relationship with the teachers of the ITP class? 8.47 *1.41*

... with your fellow participants? 8.40 *1.52*

... with your family? 7.60 *2.79*

... with your friends? 8.73 *1.17*

Overall, on a scale of 0 to 10, how successful do you feel you have been in following your commitments? 7.23 *1.81*

Absences during Cycle 93. <u>4.87</u> *2.80*

(From July 3, 1993, midterm questionnaire.) On a scale of 0 to 10, how confident are you that if you fulfill your commitments to the class you will realize your affirmations by November 20, 1993? <u>7.52</u> *1.70*

A computer analysis of the correlations between participants' answers to these questions and their success in achieving their affirmations shows statistically significant relationships as listed below. The questions are presented in condensed form. The symbol *r* stands for the correlation coefficient; the larger the *r* figure, the greater the correlation between the participants' answers and their success in achieving the affirmation. (A perfect correlation would be 1.0, but that would be practically impossible.) The *p* rating has to do with probability. The lower the *p* rating, the less probability that the correlation is due to chance. Any *p* rating of less than .05 is considered statistically significant. We are listing only the correlations that proved to be statistically significant.

**Affirmation 1**

How focused Kata imaging ($r=.381, p=.038$)
Strength training av. times/week last six months ($r=.379, p=.039$)
Faithfully completed reading ($r=.407, p=.026$)
How successful follow commitments ($r=.486, p=.006$)

**Affirmation 2**

(regarding percentage change in body fat)
Aerobic exercise minutes/week ($r=-.514, p=.004$)
Absences ($r=.437, p=.016$)

**Affirmation 3**

(metanormal)
No statistically significant correlations

**Affirmation 4**

(balanced, vital, and healthy)
How focused Kata imaging ($r=.492, p=.006$)
Aerobic exercise minutes/week ($r=.593, p=.0006$)
How conscious of what eaten ($r=.533, p=.002$)
Healthfulness of diet ($r=.541, p=.002$)
Understand theoretical underpinnings ($r=.392, p=.032$)

Staying current with significant feelings ($r$=.632, $p$=.0002)
Satisfied relationships with participants ($r$=.402, $p$=.028)
Satisfied relationships with friends ($r$=.521, $p$=.003)
How successful follow commitments ($r$=.420, $p$=.021)

**Average of Affirmations 1, 3, and 4**

How focused Kata imaging ($r$=.395, $p$=.031)
How conscious of what eaten ($r$=.386, $p$=.035)
How successful follow commitments ($r$=.401, $p$=.028)

In considering these figures, bear in mind that correlation does not prove a casual relationship. In other words, a $p$ of .028 doesn't mean that successfully following commitments had a rather good probability of *causing* participants to successfully realize Affirmations 1, 3, and 4. Cause might well be involved, but all that is proved here is a statistically significant *relationship* between successfully following commitments and realizing Affirmations 1, 3, and 4 as averaged.

This study involves certain limitations. The participants do not represent a random sample but were selected from applicants who were willing and able to pay $85 a month for the program. Nor was there a control group against which to compare results. Also bear in mind that while some answers to the questionnaires and rating of success in achieving affirmations were based on objective data, others were subjective. As stated in chapter 2, the teachers spent much time preparing participants to rate nonobjective affirmations with total integrity, avoiding either positive or negative bias. Comparing the participants' ratings against our own observations, we concluded that they were as reliable as any self-ratings could be. Despite the limitations, we believe the above correlations and probabilities can be helpful in suggesting certain tendencies that emerge from this practice.

**The Authors' Comments on the Statistical Relationship Between Adherence to the Program and Success in Achieving Affirmations**

In these comments, we use the condensed form of the items on the participant questionnaire. The full versions are carried near the beginning of this appendix.

We anticipated a connection between participants' adherence to the program and their success in realizing their affirmations. This relationship showed up in the correlation between "How successful follow commitments" and Affirmations 1 and 4, as well as the average of Affirmations 1, 3, and 4. In the 1992 Cycle, the number of times a week participants did the ITP Kata (which we consider a good marker of adherence) showed up as statistically significant as related to success in achieving Affirmation 4 and the average of all affirmations. In the 1993 Cycle, however, "Kata times per week" did not show up as statistically significant in relation to any affirmation.

Participants' consciousness, awareness, and powers of focused attention—all of which might go under the headings of "mind" and "soul"—proved especially significant in this study. Note that "How focused Kata imaging" showed up as statistically significant as related to success in achieving Affirmations 1, 4, and the average of 1, 3, and 4, while the number of times a week participants performed the Kata did not appear. "How conscious of what eaten" showed up in relation to Affirmation 4 and in the average of Affirmations 1, 3, and 4, while "Healthfulness of diet" showed up only in relation to Affirmation 4. The only three items that showed statistically significant relationships to success in achieving Affirmations 1, 3, and 4 as averaged were "How focused Kata imaging," "How conscious of what eaten," and "How successful follow commitments."

Affirmation 2 involved a purely objective measure, the percentage of reduction of body fat. An experienced exercise physiologist took caliper skin-fold measurements on March 27, 1993, then again on November 13, 1993, to determine the changes for each individual and as an average for the thirty participants. The average turned out to be a loss of 12.60 percent. The only items that related in a statistically significant way to success in achieving this loss of percentage of body fat were "Aerobic exercise minutes/week" and attendance at the Saturday morning class.

We are impressed by the strong correlation between aerobic exercise and loss of body fat and somewhat surprised by the lack of statistically significant relationships between this loss and both strength training and diet. Six participants and three teachers engaged in regular programs of strength training at a health club during 1993, and all of them showed significant losses in percentage of body fat. Certain participants adopted very-low-fat diets (see chapter 10), and they, too, showed significant body fat loss. The lack of statistically significant correlations involving these factors does not negate their importance. The strong correlation involving aerobic exercise might be at least partially accounted for by the fact that while ITP participants were committed to only three hours a week of aerobics, they averaged over four hours a week, creating a wide range of scores, which might make statistical significance easier to come by. Still, there is no question that regular aerobic exercise is an important factor, perhaps the most important factor, in a healthy reduction of body fat.

We see the correlation between number of absences and success in reducing body fat (an average loss of 12.6 percent body fat) as another suggestion of the importance of adherence to the program. Note that the correlation between body fat and absences is significantly positive in that when absences go up, body fat goes up ($r=.437$, $p=.016$). However the correlation between aerobic exercise and body fat is significantly negative, in that when exercise goes up, body fat goes down ($r=-.514$, $p=.004$).

Even though participants reported an average success of 6.67 on a scale of 0 to 10 in achieving Affirmation 3, there are no statistically significant correlations that involve this affirmation except as it figures in the average of Affirmations 1, 3, and 4. Perhaps the subjective nature of many of these affirmations made them hard to rate accurately. But this, we believe, is only part of the story. Our experience has shown us that when we deal with the realm of the metanormal, we sometimes encounter steep and unexpected inflections in the learning curve. Some of the changes simply defy analysis, and we must at least consider the possibility of grace, of extraordinary capacities that come to us as freely given rather than earned, spontaneously revealed rather than attained. Anomalies appear even with the purely objective Affirmation 2. Take the case, for example, of the participant who showed a 24.3 percent loss in body fat along with a 5.5 pound gain in lean body mass despite the fact that he changed his physical regimen not at all during the 1993 Cycle and adopted a diet high in fat two months before the second calipers measurement. We can speculate that there will always be mysteries beyond the reach of analysis. At the same time, we believe we can profit by studying these mysteries, searching for lawfulness in their operations.

We consider this statistical study preliminary and intend to refine our methods for defining and understanding what might be referred to as grace. We urge others to join in this search. We continue to assume that, as Ramakrishna said, "The winds of grace are always blowing. But we have to raise our sails." We continue to believe that a long-term integral, transformative practice is the best way to raise our sails.

In this regard, the correlations with Affirmation 4 are most encouraging. These correlations, in effect, draw a fairly complete profile of a long-term transformative practice, one that integrates body, mind, heart, and soul. "How focused Kata imaging" involves the mind and the soul, as does "How conscious of what eaten." Aerobic exercise and healthfulness of diet involve the body. "Understand theoretical underpinnings" brings the mind into play. Staying current with feelings and having satisfying personal relationships implicates the heart. And successfully following commitments speaks to a dedication to long-term practice itself, the measure of any successful, lasting transformation.

# APPENDIX  C

# *Selected Readings*

Every one of the books listed here relates in some way to the ideas and practices we have discussed. Some were written for a popular audience; others are more difficult. Some are historically important in the development of thinking about human nature, the world, and the divine, while others will eventually be replaced by more up-to-date accounts of particular discoveries, theories, or fields of inquiry. A few are currently out of print but can be found in libraries as well as stores that sell used books. All of them, we believe, will broaden your understanding of the principles supporting Integral Transformative Practice.

We recommend that you follow your own first interests in approaching this list. One book will suggest another, so you can begin with any one of them and go on to others. Many have useful bibliographies.

**Philosophy**

Sri Aurobindo. *The Life Divine.* The Sri Aurobindo Ashram, Pondicherry, India, 1981. This is the main philosophic work of the Indian philosopher noted in the preface and in chapters 1 and 12. In it, the "involution-evolution" perspective is presented with great richness and scope.

Frederick Copleston. *A History of Philosophy* (three volumes). Doubleday Image Books, 1985. An authoritative, widely acclaimed reference work on Western philosophy from the pre-Socratics to Sartre.

*The Encyclopedia of Philosophy* (four volumes). Macmillan Reprint Edition, 1972. Essays on a huge range of philosophies, ideas, and philosophers by leading authorities on the subjects addressed.

David Ray Griffin. *God and Religion in the Postmodern World.* State University of New York Press, 1989. This book includes a lucid description of Alfred North Whitehead's central philosophic ideas, which resonate strongly with the "involution-evolution" perspective.

Satprem. *Sri Aurobindo, or the Adventure of Consciousness.* India Library Society, 1964. An account of Sri Aurobindo's spiritual life, with vivid descriptions of the philosopher's metanormal experiences.

Ken Wilber. *Sex, Ecology, Spirituality: The Spirit of Evolution.* Shambhala Publications Inc., 1995. A sweeping review and critique of scientific, religious, and philosophic visions regarding universal and human evolution.

**The History of Religious Thought and Practice**

Karen Armstrong. *The History of God: The Four-Thousand Year Quest of Judaism, Christianity, and Islam.* Alfred A. Knopf Inc., 1993.

Huston Smith. *The World's Religions.* HarperSanFrancisco, 1991. A lucid, authoritative introduction to the world's religions by one of the world's leading scholars of comparative religious studies.

Philip Novak. *The World's Wisdom.* HarperSanFrancisco, 1994. A beautifully organized collection of sacred texts from Hinduism, Buddhism, Confucianism, Taoism, Judaism, Christianity, Islam, and the primal religions.

Larry Dossey, M.D. *Healing Words*. HarperSan Francisco, 1993. A survey of studies on the power of prayer, with insightful commentary by a pioneer in the interface between the scientific and the spiritual.

Hoyt L. Edge, Robert L. Morris, John Palmer, and Joseph H. Rush. *Foundations of Parapsychology: Exploring the Boundaries of Human Capability*. Routledge & Kegan Paul, 1986. A highly authoritative and comprehensive review of parapsychology and psychical research.

Caryle Hirshberg and Marc Ian Barasch. *Remarkable Recovery*. Riverhead Books, 1995. A well-informed, well-written report on the extraordinary transformations involved in what medical science calls "spontaneous remission."

William James. *Essays in Psychical Research*. Harvard University Press, 1986. These still-illuminating essays in many cases go beyond the standard thinking in contemporary parapsychology.

William James. *The Varieties of Religious Experience*. Random House Inc., 1902 and 1993. A comparative study of religious experience by America's most prominent psychologist-philosopher. James combines a deep appreciation of religious experience with critical distance from theological and philosophic interpretations of them. His approach, like that of Frederic Myers and Abraham Maslow (see below), constitutes a "natural history" of extraordinary functioning and exemplifies the open-minded but discriminating attitude we need in order to understand the complexities of integral transformation.

Abraham Maslow. *Toward a Psychology of Being*. Second Edition. Van Nostrand, 1968. *The Farther Reaches of Human Nature*. Viking Compass, 1971. Two collections of essays about our possibilities for further development. Maslow was a founder of humanistic and transpersonal psychology, and, like William James, helped broaden psychology's embrace of extraordinary human functioning.

Frederic Myers. *Human Personality, and Its Survival of Bodily Death*. Longmans, Green, 1903 and 1954. A comprehensive, richly detailed account of pathological, normal, and metanormal phenom-

**Studies of Metanormal Experience**

ena that reveal latent powers of mind and body. Myers invented the word "telepathy," was a principal founder of psychical research, and strongly influenced William James, Carl Jung, and other leading students of human nature. For further information about paranormal phenomena, see Edmund Gurney: *Phantasms of the Living*, Scholars' Facsimiles & Reprints, 1970. Gurney was a colleague of Myers and a pioneer of psychical research.

Herbert Thurston, S. J. *The Physical Phenomena of Mysticism*. Burns Oates, 1952.

**Cosmology**

Paul Davies. *The Mind of God*. Simon & Schuster, 1992. A popular exploration of the mysteries inherent in the laws of mathematics and physics, by a respected mathematical physicist.

George Greenstein. *The Symbiotic Universe*. William Morrow & Co. Inc., 1988. A description of apparent coincidences in the development of the universe without which life would never have developed.

Michio Kaku. *Hyperspace: A Scientific Odyssey Through Parallel Universes, Time Warps, and the 10th Dimension*. Oxford University Press, 1994. An illuminating primer on physical theory, culminating in speculations on higher-dimensional space–time concepts that might someday unify all of nature's fundamental forces into one comprehensive theory.

Joseph Silk. *The Big Bang* (revised edition). W. H. Freeman, and Co. 1989. An account of standard thinking about the universe's birth and early origins.

**Evolutionary Theory**

David Deamer and Gail Fleischauer. *Origins of Life: The Central Concepts*. Jones & Bartlett Publishers Inc., 1994. A comprehensive review of research discoveries and current theory regarding life's origins.

Monroe Strickberger (editor). *Evolution.* Jones & Bartlett Publishers Inc., 1990. A good overview of the progression of our scientific understanding of life's evolution on earth.

Jonathon Weiner. *The Beak of the Finch.* Alfred A. Knopf Inc., 1994. A delightful book showing that, under certain conditions, biological evolution can move much faster than Darwin—or anyone else—believed possible.

Peter Farb. *Humankind.* Houghton Mifflin Co., 1978. A wide-ranging popular account of discoveries in modern anthropology.

**Anthropology and Pre-Civilized Human History**

Robert Jurmain, Harry Nelson, and Williams A. Turnbaugh. *Understanding Physical Anthropology and Archeology.* West Publishing Co., 1987. A standard college text that combines physical anthropology with archeology.

Roger Lewin. *In the Age of Mankind.* Smithsonian Institution Press, 1988. A Smithsonian book of human evolution in a beautifully illustrated coffee-table format.

J. Benthall and Ted Polhemus (editors). *The Body As a Medium of Expression.* Allen, Lane & Dutton, 1975. Ted Polhemus (editor). *The Body Reader: Social Aspects of the Human Body.* Pantheon Books, 1978. Collections of essays about the interplay of cultural norms, institutions, and bodily functioning. These essays reveal the pervasiveness of social influences on our carriage, gestures, facial expressions, body image, somatic structure, health, and exercise patterns.

**Sociological and Anthropological Studies of Culture's Influence on Individual Development**

Pierre Bourdieu: *Distinction: A Social Critique of the Judgement of Taste.* Harvard University Press, 1984. Studies of cultural influences (primarily French) on fashion, lifestyle, class tastes, body image, status, sense of entitlement, permitted pleasures, and other aspects of human life.

Mary Douglas. *Purity and Danger: An Analysis of Concepts of Pollution and Taboo.* Penguin Books, 1970. Case studies and analyses of society's influence on our concepts of cleanliness, dirtiness, and acceptable physical activity. Douglas helped pioneer the study of the body's cultural shaping.

Stephen Katz (editor). *Mysticism and Philosophical Analysis.* Oxford University Press, 1978. Stephen Katz (editor). *Mysticism and Religious Traditions.* Oxford University Press, 1983. Essays arguing that our religious philosophies, which are culturally shaped, determine the kind of religious experience we have. Katz maintains that mystical experience, like all other human experience, is molded by our socially acquired beliefs.

**General Health**    William Evans, Ph.D., and Irwin H. Rosenberg, M.D. *Biomarkers.* Simon & Schuster, 1991. Ostensibly about controlling the ill effects of aging, this book makes powerful arguments for the benefits of aerobic and strength exercise at every stage of life.

Dean Ornish, M.D. *Dr. Dean Ornish's Program for Reversing Heart Disease.* Random House Inc., 1990. Designed as a guide to reversing or preventing heart disease, this landmark book also serves as a reliable guide to the general good health of mind, body, heart, and soul for everyone.

# About the Authors

GEORGE LEONARD, a pioneer in the field of human potential, is author of twelve books, including *The Transformation, Education and Ecstasy, The Ultimate Athlete*, and *Mastery*. During his seventeen years as senior editor for *Look* magazine, he won an unprecedented number of national awards for education writing, and during the 1980s produced annual *Ultimate Fitness* sections for *Esquire*, as well as numerous articles on a wide variety of subjects in such magazines as *Esquire, Harper's, Atlantic, New York, Saturday Review*, and *The Nation*.

Leonard holds a fifth-degree black belt in aikido, and is co-owner of a martial arts school in Mill Valley, California. He is founder of Leonard Energy Training (LET), a transformative practice inspired by aikido, which he has introduced to some 50,000 people in the United States and abroad. He is a past president of the Association for Humanistic Psychology, and is currently president of the Board of Esalen Institute.

MICHAEL MURPHY founded Esalen Institute (with Richard Price) in 1962 and helped start Esalen's Russian-American Exchange Program. Through this work, he helped create a new style of citizens' diplomacy that increased understanding between the two superpowers at a historic moment. Murphy currently serves as chairman of the Board of the Esalen Institute.

Murphy is the author of four novels, *Golf in the Kingdom, The Kingdom of Shivas Irons, Jacob Atabet*, and *An End to Ordinary History*, in addition to four works of nonfiction, *The Future of the Body, In the Zone: Transcendent Experience in Sport* (with Rhea White), *God and the Evolving Universe* (with James Redfield and Sylvia Timbers), and *The Physical and Psychological Effects of Meditation* (with Steven Donovan and Margaret Livingston)